# Capital Punishment in American Courts

**James Biser Whisker
and Kevin Spiker**

# Capital Punishment in American Courts

**James Biser Whisker
and Kevin Spiker**

Academica Press
Washington - London

Library of Congress Cataloging-in-Publication Data

Names: Whisker, James B., 1939- author. | Spiker, Kevin, author.
Title: Capital punishment in American courts / James Biser Whisker,
Kevin Spiker.
Description: Washington : Academica Press, 2020. | Includes
bibliographical references and index. | Summary: "In the 400 years since
the first known execution was carried out for treason in Virginia,
American jurisdictions have debated both the appropriateness and
methods of capital punishment and placed varying restrictions on its
application. This book surveys this history from a penetrating new
perspective"-- Provided by publisher.
Identifiers: LCCN 2019046171 | ISBN 9781680532050 (hardcover) |
ISBN 9781680532180 (paperback)
Subjects: LCSH: Capital punishment--United States. | Capital
punishment--United States--Cases. | Discrimination in capital
punishment--United States. | Discrimination in criminal justice
administration--United States.
Classification: LCC KF9227.C2 W43 2020 | DDC 345.73/0773--dc23
LC record available at https://lccn.loc.gov/2019046171

James Biser Whisker is Professor Emeritus at West Virginia University, where he taught for over 37 years. He was adviser to the WVU College Republicans for most of his tenure. He received his Ph. D. in 1969 from the University of Marland. He is author or co-author of books on gunsmiths and arms makers in eighteen states. He has co-authored books on clockmakers and silversmiths of Pennsylvania and Maryland. Among his other books are *The Alien Tort Claims Act, The Militia, The Right to Hunt; The Citizen-Soldier and U.S. Military Policy, Our Vanishing Freedom: The Right to Keep and Bear Arms, and the Rise and Decline of the American Militia System*. He currently resides in Everett, West Virginia with his wife of 48 years, the former Sheila Elaine Bailey.

Kevin Spiker is Associate Professor of Political Science at Ohio University Eastern where he teaches classes in American government, political theory, elections and political parties, and the American presidency. He received his Ph.D. in political science from West Virginia University in 2003. Among his other books are: *Erskine S. Allin, Director of the U.S. Armory in Springfield, Massachusetts*, and with Dr. Whisker, *The Alien Tort Claims Act*.

.

# Contents

# Introduction

Few debates in American society invoke more debates, and divide participants more, than capital punishment. Many American states have abandoned its use and others, while nominally still allowing for its legal imposition, have realistically abandoned it. Languishing on death row in many states are more than three thousand persons convicted of capital crimes. Most of these condemned persons are in some stage of appeal.

When we prepared our first volume on this issue one of my former students, now an accomplished defense attorney, said to me that he favored capital punishment, much to my great surprise. His reasons for preferring executions to life imprisonment were very different than my own. He said he loathed the vision of a man, say, in his twenties, convicted of a capital crime, languishing in a tiny six by eight foot cage for perhaps the next sixty years without any but false hope that one day he might be free. That, he said, was indeed cruel and unusual punishment. In its essence it differed little from the ancient and medieval punishment of dumping an accused person in a dark dungeon and, except for feeding and occasional cleansing, forgetting about him until he died.

The proponents of capital punishment in the United States have been focusing their attention of two major concerns: those who commit what crimes can be subject to execution, and what method[s] of execution can be used?

First, let us consider the methods of execution. Many proponents do not agree with the late brilliant Justice Antonin Scalia (1936—2016) that those to be executed have no right to a painless execution. The courts, minus Justice Scalia, have been concerned with this question. Thus far it has not appeared in federal litigation perhaps because the federal government has executed so few criminals and perhaps in part because the federal agents used lethal injections, presumed to be the least painful method.

In earlier times the nations of the world sought to employ the most painful method of execution. Even a simple explanation of some of these executions offend sensitivities of many. A short list of such painful executions include: roasting alive, boiling alive, drawing and quartering, sawing in half, flaying alive, and disembowelment. Even the Hebrew Bible mentions burning alive and stoning to death. A few brutal methods have survived in the Islamic world and among more primitive nations.

Hanging has long been the preferred method of execution. In earlier times prisoners were drawn upward, much like raising the flag on a pole. Death was prolonged and criminals died by asphyxiation. A certain Sergeant Hickey led a plot to assassinate General George Washington early in the First War for Independence. It took eighteen minutes for him to die. Later, prisoners were dropped from a height and immediate death was supposed to occur by dislocation of the neck. That did not always occur and once again the condemned died by strangulation. At the Nuremberg executions in 1948 Sergeant John Wood, some say on purpose, failed to locate the rope correctly and the condemned Nazi war criminals took as long as twenty-six minutes to slowly strangle to death.

As man began to master electricity and harness it for good some employed it for executions. While many condemned were killed upon the first shock, others lingered and required additional shocks. We shall see later the executions of Julius and Ethel Rosenberg for espionage. Julius died immediately but Ethel required several bursts and her body was seen smoking by the time enough shock had been administered. Improper procedure can, and in some cases did, cause the infliction of considerable pain and suffering.

Likewise, the gas chamber was devised as a less painful, and more certain, method of execution than hanging. Reports of the accidental infliction of pain caused several states to abandon the gas chamber. Another factor in the desertion of gas chambers was the execution of many millions using Zyklon B gas in Nazi death camps.

Presently, nearly all executions are carried out using lethal injections. The exact cocktail has varied, but essentially the condemned is put to sleep and then executed. But botched executions as well as difficulty in finding veins to inject with the drugs has called this method into question as well.

Utah is the only state that has allowed in recent times the use of the firing squad. Several shooters are provided with weapons, commonly .30 caliber rifles. with one rifle containing a blank cartridge. The shooters are instructed to aim for the heart where a white patch is placed. As we shall see, this was a common method of public execution used by various armies. The U.S. Army executed Eddie Slovik for desertion. The execution team fired shots that hit him in the heart, the next, and even the shoulder. Those who are film buffs may recall the execution of three of its own soldiers charged with cowardice in the face of the enemy by the French high command, in Stanley Kubrick's 1957 film *Paths of Glory.*

It would seem highly unlikely that modern nations would return to beheading although this was the common method of execution in pre-World War II Europe. On 10 October 1789, Joseph-Ignace Guillotin, a French physician, proposed to the National Assembly that capital punishment should always take the form of decapitation by means of a simple mechanism designed to behead the condemned. Guillotin, together with German engineer Tobias Schmidt, built a prototype for the guillotine. Schmidt recommended using an angled blade as opposed to a round one and this would make death certain. Dr. Guillotin argued persuasively that decapitation would be essentially painless. The world wide net has several sites that show actual decapitations by the guillotine. We did not discover any instances in the United States where beheading was employed.

Let us return to the question of when capital punishment should be employed. We can immediately dismiss a wide variety of religious transgressions. Distasteful as sacrilege may be this must be rejected in modern secular states. Of course sacrilege may still invoke capital punishment in states where religion and political power are inseparably intertwined, as in many Islamic nations.

Ancient Israel was a theocracy and thus certain violations of religious taboos could invoke capital punishment. Some of the essentially religious transgressions calling for the death penalty in the Hebrew Bible are: worshiping false gods; false prophecy; necromancy; violating the Sabbath; practicing witchcraft; blasphemy; intrusion in the temple by a foreigner; sacrifices, especially human sacrifice, to false gods; bestiality; male homosexuality; and prostitution by a daughter of a priest. Neither modern Israel nor Christian nations which place great emphasis on the Hebrew Bible follow these proscriptions, let alone use them to invoke capital punishment.

In the United States at the national level there are crimes that are inappropriate for legislative concern at the state level. Treason and spying or espionage have long been considered capital crimes by virtually every nation, at least until the modern rejection of all capital punishment in Europe. As we shall see, Julius and Ethel Rosenberg were executed for stealing state secrets, especially as related to nuclear power and the atomic bomb. However, executions for spying are few and far between in the United States. Most spying has involved prison sentences and occasional exchanges of their spies for our spies.

Certain international crimes carry universal condemnation and as such may be prosecuted by any nation. Piracy was the principal crime so recognized at the time of the adoption of the U.S. Constitution. One of the more unusual applications of capital punishment for piracy was the execution of captains of slave trading vessels. Currently it may be applied to air piracy as well as piracy on the high seas.

The execution of Eddie Slovik on 31 January 1945 for desertion was unique in the United States in World War II. Commonly, desertion was punished by a prison sentence. During the American Civil War the North executed literally dozens of men for desertion. This remains a possibility to this day.

During World War II all military branches of the United States executed men for rape and murder. The United States Army carried out 141 executions over a three-year period from 1942-45 and a further six executions were conducted during the postwar period, for a known total of 147. It had official hangmen, such as Sergeant John Wood who later hanged Nazi war criminals at Nuremberg. These were executed by hanging.

States that utilize capital as the highest form of punishment seem limited to certain types of murder. One can make out some very strong arguments for capital punishment for aggravated rape among other non-murder charges. Victims of brutal rapes frequently lose much of their human personality and occasionally physical functioning. Likewise extreme physical mutilation, such as blinding or destruction of limbs, would seem to cry out for execution of the perpetrator. U.S. Supreme Court guidelines restrict the death sentence to aggravated murder.

Among the constitutional applications of the death sentence are murders of police officers, jail guards, and certain similar law enforcement personnel. The rationale here is exactly the same as are the reasons for making super-human efforts to catch those who killed police officers: such a person who attacks an armed policeman would not hesitate in taking on a presumably unarmed civilian. Moreover, a person in prison for life without the possibility of parole cannot be punished more legally unless the state imposes the death sentence.

Most other constitutionally permitted capital cases involve some level of extreme brutality and/or multiple killings. Murder of a rape victim, extreme abuse of a corpse, torture before killing, are among the cases in which states have been allowed to impose the death sentence.

Should major drug traffickers may be executed under federal law. The War on Drugs is a complex ordeal with a far-reaching and profound impact on society. While citizens buckle under the weight of drug crimes and addiction, politicians hijacked the theme to project a tough-on-crime image to the public while doing little to solve the problems. President Trump joined a long line of his predecessors when he held a War on Drugs speech of his own. "We're wasting our time if we don't get tough with drug dealers, and that toughness includes the death penalty," he told an audience in New Hampshire on March 19. "The ultimate penalty has to be the death penalty." The President's words echoed earlier statements of support for Rodrigo Duterte, President of the Philippines, who has been waging a brutal war on drug dealers and users since he came to power in June of 2016. Dubbed Operation Double Barrel, Duterte's war has resulted in the extrajudicial execution of more than 12,000 people accused of using and selling drugs across the Philippines.

Why not allow the states also to do the same with major drug dealers that they encounter? When one considers how many lives are taken or destroyed otherwise by drug use, is there no justification for executing the major importers and suppliers? It might be difficult to find anyone who truly opposes the death sentence for drug overlords. We might refer back to Judge Kauffman's words to the Rosenberg's as he imposed the death sentence on them. They killed no one personally, but what they did in supply our enemies with atomic secrets killed many. The main difference would be that most, if not all, major drug traffickers have indeed ordered numerous killings. For example, Griselda Blanco, "the Godmother of Cocaine," reportedly was responsible for the homicides of 200 people in Colombia, Florida, New York, and California. Another drug kingpin was Jorge Alberto Rodríguez, also known as Don Cholito. He was a notorious Puerto Rican drug lord who hails from the Bronx, New York, who imported as much as 12,500 kilograms (27,600 pounds) of cocaine into the U.S. every month. He was also infamous for ordering numerous murders of informants, witnesses, and law-enforcement officials in the U.S. and Colombia.

The principal objection many have to capital punishment is its failure to prevent crimes that carry execution as the ultimate punishment. One who is condemned to die for a crime will most likely never actually be executed. If that condemned person is executed it will be only at the end of a prolonged process of appeals, scheduled and then canceled execution dates, and endless inquiries and testing. Its uncertainty obviates its deterrent value.

While it is undeniably true that prejudice was such that a person of color was more likely to be scheduled for execution than a white person, there are two immediate considerations we must examine. First, was what the condemned person was convicted of truly worthy of capital punishment? Second, did the condemned person have full access to complete legal counsel?

With a full array of free legal services, the imposition of law students eager to find a mistaken conviction, the American Civil Liberties

Union, and a host of other legal aid institutions and organizations, each questionable conviction can be completely scrutinized. A full range of testing and analysis of evidence is available. Thus, it is more likely that a person condemned to death will have more assistance by far than a person consigned to life without parole. We will look at the infamous Scottsboro case and note that legal assistance ended abruptly when the sentences were changed from execution to life without parole.

# Early Capital Cases
# in the U. S. Supreme Court

Capital punishment, also known as the death penalty, is a government-sanctioned practice whereby a person is killed by the state as a punishment for a crime. The sentence that someone be punished in such a manner is referred to as a death sentence, whereas the act of carrying out the sentence is known as an execution. Crimes that are punishable by death are known as capital crimes or capital offenses, and they commonly include offenses such as murder, treason, espionage, war crimes, and crimes against humanity and genocide. Etymologically, the term capital in this context alluded to execution by beheading.[1]

The first known infliction of the death penalty in the American colonies occurred in Jamestown Colony in 1608. The first execution in the New World took place in Virginia in 1608 when Captain George Kendall was executed in Jamestown for spying for Spain. In 1612, Virginia governor Thomas Dale enacted the Divine, Moral and Martial Laws, which provided the death penalty for even minor offenses such as stealing grapes, killing chickens, and trading with Indians. In 1623 Daniel Frank was condemned to hang for theft in the Jamestown colony. This was the first hanging to take place in what became the United States. In 1632 Jane Champion was the first woman executed in the United States.

Death penalty laws varied considerably from colony to colony. There were a total of 162 known death sentences carried out in all the

---

[1] Wikipedia entry for Capital punishment.

colonies during the seventeenth century. Several relatively minor offenses such as striking one's mother or father or denying the "true God," were punishable by death. During the 1600s there was a total of five documented death sentences handed down in the colonies for same-sex sodomy: two each in Connecticut and New York, and one in Virginia.[2] There was an additional prosecution in New York for which records do not show disposition of the case, making the five known for same-sex sodomy.[3]

The Massachusetts Bay Colony held its first execution in 1630, although the Capital Laws of New England did not go into effect until many years later. Using death as a punishment was common in the state's earliest days. In one notable case, Mary Dyer, was put to death in Boston in 1660 after she was banned by the Puritan leaders of the Massachusetts Bay Colony for being a member of the Society of Friends. Dyer returned several times in defiance of the colony's anti-Quaker laws and was eventually hanged.[4] Capital punishment reached a new fervor a few decades later, when 19 people were hanged and one person crushed to death during the 1692 Salem witch trials. During the Salem Witch Trials, most of the men and women convicted of witchcraft were sentenced to public hanging. It is generally accepted that that seventeen women and two men were hanged as a result of the trials. However, one modern scholar

---

[2] According to *Executions in the U.S. 1608-1987: The Espy File, which is* not documented, there were ten known executions for sodomy or buggery in the colonies between 1625 and 1674. This included same-sex or different sex, human-human or human-beast, or act type unspecified). One of those executions occurred in Virginia, two in New York, three in Massachusetts, and four in Connecticut. Between 1757 and 1801 there were five executions for sodomy or buggery. Three were in New Jersey, one in Pennsylvania, and one under Spanish law in California. The site DeathPenalty.ProCon cites the Espy File as listing a total of 15 colonial-era executions for "sodomy/buggery/bestiality." There are claims not in the Espy File of three more death sentences carried out for sodomy between 1692 and 1743 with one each in New Jersey, Massachusetts, and Georgia.

[3] Paternoster, Raymond. *Capital Punishment in America.* New York: Lexington, 1991, p. 4.

[4] A statue of Dyer now stands in front of the Statehouse as a warning against religious intolerance.

asserted that thousands of individuals were hanged for witchcraft throughout the American colonies.[5]

Cesare Beccaria's 1767 essay, *On Crimes and Punishment,* had an especially strong impact on legal thinking in the new world. In the essay, Beccaria theorized that there was no justification for the state's taking of a life. This brilliant essay provided legal scholars with an authoritative voice. Legal analysts saw that one result of Beccaria was the abolition of the death penalty in Austria and Tuscany.

American intellectuals were greatly influenced by Beccaria. No less an American scholar than Thomas Jefferson attempted to revise his native Virginia's death penalty laws. The bill proposed that capital punishment be used only for the crimes of murder and treason. It failed passage by a single vote.

Equally influenced by Beccaria was Dr. Benjamin Rush of Byberry, Philadelphia County, distinguished physician, signer of the Declaration of Independence and founder of the Pennsylvania Prison Society. Dr. Rush found in Beccaria strong support for his own belief that the death penalty fails to serve as a deterrent. Indeed, Dr. Rush was an early adherent to the so-called "brutalization effect." He held that having a death penalty actually increased criminal conduct. Dr. Rush gained the support of Benjamin Franklin and Philadelphia Attorney General William Bradford. Bradford, who would later become the U.S. Attorney General, led Pennsylvania to become the first state to consider degrees of murder based on culpability. In 1794, Pennsylvania repealed the death penalty for all offenses except first degree murder. In 1834, Pennsylvania became the first state to move executions away from the public eye, carrying them out in correctional facilities.

In the early to mid-Nineteenth Century, many states reduced the number of their capital crimes. This was accompanied by the construction of state penitentiaries. In 1834, Pennsylvania became the first state to move executions away from the public eye and carrying them out in correctional facilities. In 1846, Michigan became the first state to abolish

---

[5] Stack, Richard A. *Dead Wrong: Violence, Vengeance, and the Victims of Capital Punishment.* Greenwood Publishing Group, 2006.

the death penalty for all crimes except treason. Later, Rhode Island and Wisconsin abolished the death penalty for all crimes.

Although a few U.S. states moved away from the death penalty, most states held onto capital punishment. Indeed some states made more crimes capital offenses. This was especially for offenses committed by slaves in the ante-bellum South. In 1838, in an effort to make the death penalty more palatable to the public, some states began passing laws against mandatory death sentencing instead enacting discretionary death penalty statutes. This introduction of sentencing discretion in the capital process was perceived as a victory for civil libertarians because prior to the enactment of these statutes, all states mandated the death penalty for anyone convicted of a capital crime, irrespective of the circumstances. Essentially, all mandatory capital punishment laws had been abolished by 1963.

In the time span beginning in the 1920s through the 1940s, there was a resurgence in the use of the death penalty. The main factor can be seen in the writings of a new wave of criminologists who argued that the death penalty was both a necessary and useful social measure. Because of the very public crime wave that accompanied Prohibition, Americans demanded a heavy dose of law and order with the imposition of significant penalties for the criminal element. There were more executions in the 1930s than in any other decade in American history, an average of 167 per year.

Early cases heard before the United States Supreme Court focused on very few matters. The question of the nature and composition of cruel and unusual punishment focused entirely on those methods of punishment that had long been abandoned in Western Civilization. Likewise, what constituted double jeopardy was narrowly construed. However, the requirement for legal assistance to indigent poor defendants charged with capital offenses was not discovered until the fourth decade of the twentieth century. Questions of race were ignored through the middle of that same century.

# Evolving Standards of Decency

The Eighth Amendment to the United States Constitution proscribes "punishments which are incompatible with 'the evolving standards of decency that mark the progress of a maturing society.'"[6] In evaluating whether these standards of decency are met the court must consider whether: the punishment is cruel or involves torture or a lingering death;[7] and whether it involves the unnecessary and wanton infliction of pain. [8] Additionally, "no court would approve any method of implementation of the death sentence found to involve unnecessary cruelty in light of presently available alternatives."[9] The Eighth Amendment does not require states to adopt the most humane method of execution.[10]

In 1910 the Supreme Court observed that the concept of cruel and unusual punishment "is not fastened to the obsolete, but may acquire meaning as public opinion becomes enlightened by a humane justice."[11] This was found to be so even before the rigors of the Eighth Amendment were applied to the states.[12]

In 1947 the high court had written, "Taking human life by unnecessarily cruel means shocks the most fundamental instincts of civilized man. It should not be possible under the constitutional procedure of a self-governing people. . . The all -important consideration is that the execution shall be so instantaneous and substantially painless that the punishment shall be reduced, as nearly as possible, to no more than that of death itself."[13]

Section 1983 of Title 42 of the *United States Code* is the basis for most suits brought in federal court against local governments and against state and local government officers to redress violations of federal law. To

---

[6] *Estelle v. Gamble,* 429 U.S. 97, 102, 97 S. Ct. 285, 290 quoting *Trop v. Dulles,* 356 U.S. 86, 101, 78 S. Ct. 590, 598 (1958).
[7] *In re Kemmler,*136 U.S. 436, 447, 10 S. Ct. 930 (1980)
[8] *Gregg v. Georgia,* 428 U.S. 153, 173, 96 S. Ct. 2909 (1976)
[9] *Furman v. Georgia,* 408 U.S. 238, 430, 92 S. Ct. 2726 (1972)
[10] *Fierro v. Gomez,* 790 F. Supp. 966 (1996)
[11] *Weems v. United States,* 217 U.S. 349 (1910).
[12] *Robinson v. California,* 370 U.S. 660 (1962).
[13] *Louisiana ex rel. Francis v. Resweber,* 329 U.S. 459 (1947)

state a claim under 1983,[14] a plaintiff must allege two essential elements: first, a violation of a right secured by the Constitution or federal laws; and, second that the alleged violation was committed by a person acting under color of state law. There is an exception to the general rule that section 1983 may be used to challenge the unconstitutionality of the actions of state officials. This exception involves challenges to the fact or duration of confinement, which must be brought by way of a petition for a writ of habeas corpus. Despite this exception, section 1983 is the basis for virtually all constitutional rulings involving the action of state and local officials.[15] The *Sullivan* court explicitly held that cases challenging the method of execution of a death sentence can be brought under section 1983.[16]

The high court did not find that changing the method of execution constituted cruel and unusual punishment. The petitioner, a murderer convicted without recommendation of mercy, was initially scheduled to be hanged. South Carolina changed its method of execution to electrocution. The Supreme Court offered this perspective. "The statute under consideration did not change the penalty-death-for murder, but only the mode of producing this, together with certain nonessential details in respect of surroundings. The punishment was not increased, and some of the odious features incident to the old method were abated."[17]

The 2008 case of *Baze v Rees* evoked several approaches to the constitutionality of the death penalty and when and if it is permitted. Writing the opinion of the Court the Chief Justice of the United States observed, "Some risk of pain is inherent in any method of execution—no matter how humane—if only from the prospect of error in following the required procedure. It is clear, then, that the Constitution does not demand the avoidance of all risk of pain in carrying out executions."[18] Justice Scalia in concurrence wrote, "I take no position on the desirability of the

---

[14] 42 U.S.C. § 1983
[15] Chemerinsky, E. *Federal Jurisdiction.* 5th ed.; Aspen, 2007, 371.
[16] *Sullivan v. Dugger,* 721 F.2d 719, 720 (11th Cir.1983), regarding 42 U.S.C. § 1983,
[17] *Malloy v South Carolina*, 237 U.S. 180 (1915)
[18] *Baze v. Rees,* 553 U.S. 35 (2008)

death penalty, except to say that its value is eminently debatable and the subject of deeply, indeed passionately, held views—which means, to me, that it is preeminently not a matter to be resolved here. And especially not when it is explicitly permitted by the Constitution." Justice Thomas wrote that a "method of execution violates the Eighth Amendment only if it is deliberately designed to inflict pain. . . ." In dissent Justice Stevens said, "The risk of executing innocent defendants can be entirely eliminated by treating any penalty more severe than life imprisonment without the possibility of parole as constitutionally excessive."

# African-Americans
# and Capital Punishment

In the early years of the Republic, as in colonial times, slaves were totally excluded from juries, as were indentured servants during the time of their servitude. Few free blacks would have been summoned for jury duty, even if the defendant was black. In the South all blacks were essentially exuded from any aspect of the court system. Even as accused slaves had no real standing or rights in court.

One aspect of prejudiced against black Americans involves their exclusion from juries. Prosecutors have long believed that all-white juries are more likely to convict and harshly sentence black defendants than are racially diverse juries. Once the U.S. Supreme Court became involved in this issue following the Fourteenth Amendment to the U.S. Constitution the exclusion of blacks from juries was disguised. Those prosecutors who excluded non-whites have long known that they can win as long as they assert that there was some reason other than race for the strike. Skilled prosecutors in practice give the actual reason for striking the potential juror, not one prepared by another else long before trial. Trial judges have routinely accepted these reasons and have usually declared that there was no conscious act of discrimination. In fact, the North Carolina Conference of District Attorneys presented a statewide training course in 1995 that included a handout called *Batson Justifications: Articulating Juror Negatives*, listing 10 modes of justifications that can be offered as racially-neutral explanations for the exclusion of potential jurors. Similar handouts have appeared in other states among prosecurial gatherings. One study conducted in 2012 in North Carolina found that eligible black jurors had been struck at twice the rate of whites. An earlier study conducted in 2003 in Louisiana study found that striking of prospective black jurors occurred at three times the rate for whites.

## The Case of Slaves

What was perhaps the first slave revolt in the South involved not only black slaves, but some indentured servants and convict laborers, and took place in Gloucester County, Virginia, in September 1663. Someone, perhaps a servant, betrayed the conspiracy, leaders were arrested, and several conspirators were beheaded. In 1739 approximately 90 slaves broke into militia stores in Stoenoe, between Charleston and Port Royal, South Carolina. The South Carolina Militia engaged the slave army and met with heavy resistance before overcoming them. Incidents like this and the other bloody slave insurrections like those led by Nat Turner and Denmark Vesey although striking hard blows at the institution of slavery also created fear in the white population. [19] Escaped slaves in 1739 attempted to march toward Spanish Florida, but were confronted by a white militia. A battle ensued in which 44 blacks and 21 whites perished. [20]

One major slave revolt in the South was led by a twenty-four year old slave named Gabriel Prosser. In early 1800, he began to lay plans to take the city of Richmond, Virginia, by force. He planned to invade Richmond, attack the state armory, and arm the rebel slaves. By August 1800, he had many slaves enlisted and had stored up an armory of weapons, including guns. Two followers betrayed him along with over a thousand followers who were ready to attack Richmond. The state militia attacked him the next day and he and his followers were hanged.

In 1802 North Carolina hanged 22 slaves for their participation in a slave revolt. On January 8 to 10, 1811, a slave rebellion occurred in Louisiana in which 500 slaves took part and 100 were killed. Other bloody slave insurrections like those led by Nat Turner and Denmark Vesey struck hard blows at the institution of slavery simultaneously creating fear in the

---

[19] http://www.lostblacklegion.org/page4.html
[20] Stephens, William, ed. *Proceedings in Georgia,* Ann Arbor: University of Michigan, 1966, 2: 128f.

white population. On the one instance a slave, who knew the entire plot, betrayed Vesey who was tried and was executed among the twenty-two insurrectionists on the 26 July 1822.

Nat Turner's Rebellion, also known as the Southampton Insurrection, was a slave rebellion that took place in Southampton County, Virginia during August 1831. Led by Nat Turner, rebellious slaves killed from 55 to 65 people, at least 51 being white. The state militia quelled rebellion within a few days. The state executed 56 slaves accused of being part of the rebellion. Militia and mobs murdered an additional 120 slaves and free blacks. Severed heads lined fence posts for months after.

Slaves, and indeed many free blacks, were not entitled to trial by jury. Most were brought before a magistrate on information supplied by whites. They were rarely allowed to summon witnesses on their behalf, have advice or representation by legal counsel, or allowed to testify. While very rarely tortured, as slaves commonly were in the ancient and medieval worlds, they were nonetheless strangers to due process. Since jury trials occurred only in the most uncommon cases, blacks did not serve on juries for their fellow blacks. In the rare case where a free black was given a jury trial there would be no blacks on the jury. There was no appeal of sentences. Capital punishment was common and often imposed for acts that were not capital crimes for whites. Methods of execution included burning, decapitation, and hanging in chains.

Owners of executed slaves were commonly reimbursed for the slave's value at the slave market via vouchers paid for by public taxation. In Virginia between 1774 and 1864 there were some thirteen hundred vouchers, each recording the conviction of one or more slaves for a capital crime along with reimbursement of the slave's owner. Of the 1117 offenses which were clearly stated, 346 were murder, discriminated as follows: murder of master, 56; of overseer, 7; of other white man, 98; of mistress, 11; of other white woman, 13; of master's child, 2; of other white child, 7; of free negro man, 7; of slave man, 59; of slave woman, 14; of slave child, 12, all of which were murders by slave women of their own children; of persons not described, 60. Of the murderers 307 were men and 39 were women.[21] Statistics are similar in other Southern states.[22]

## *Strauder v. West Virginia*

The *Strauder* decision was a United States Supreme Court case concerning racial discrimination and United States constitutional criminal procedure. *Strauder* was the first instance where the Supreme Court reversed a state court decision denying a defendant's motion to remove his criminal trial to federal court pursuant to Section 3 of the Civil Rights Act of 1866.[23]

On the morning of 18 April 1872 Taylor Strauder, a former slave, murdered his wife Anna, bludgeoning her to death with two strikes from a hatchet handle to her head. The couple had been arguing with her through the night about Anna's alleged marital infidelity. Strauder was arrested and arraigned in the Ohio County, West Virginia, Circuit Court. Strauder demurred the indictment, alleging it was defective, but the court overruled the motion. Strauder then pleaded not guilty and asked the court for a continuance which he received.

In 1872 the State of West Virginia had adopted a new state constitution. The reconstructed state court procedure provided criminal defendants with preliminary examinations. At the May 1873 term of the circuit court, Strauder made a motion requesting this examination but the Ohio County court denied the motion. The case then proceeded to trial and the jury returned a verdict of guilty and the court sentenced Strauder to death by hanging.

On appeal to the Supreme Court of West Virginia that high court held that, since Strauder's trial had not yet commenced trial at the time of the passage of the statute that provided for a preliminary examination before trial, the statute did apply to Strauder.

The state legislature had passed an additional act as part of the 1873 reconstruction of the West Virginia courts. That legislation provided

---

[21] Phillips, Ulrich B., "Slave Crime in Virginia." *American Historical Review* 20 [January 1915]: 336-40.

[22] See for example Byrne, William A., "Slave Crime in Savannah, Georgia" *The Journal of Negro History*, Vol. 79, [1994]

[23] *Strauder v. West Virginia,* 100 U.S. 303 (1880)

"[a]ll white male persons, who are twenty-one years of age and not over sixty, and who are citizens of this State, shall be liable to serve as jurors, except as herein provided." The only exception provided regarded service as a state official. Upon his case returning to the circuit court of Ohio County in November 1874, Strauder entered a motion to remove the case to federal court on grounds that blacks although they were American citizens were precluded by West Virginia law from grand and petit jury service. The West Virginia court denied the challenge. Strauder then in turn entered motions challenging the racial composition of the jury pool and the consequent racial composition of the impaneled jury. These motions were denied, the trial commenced, and the all-white jury again convicted Strauder. The trial court in January 1875 again sentenced Strauder to death by hanging.

The Supreme Court of West Virginia relied on the opinion of the Supreme Court of the United States in *The Slaughterhouse Cases* and *Bradwell v. Illinois* to find the Fourteenth Amendment had not been "intended to protect the citizens of any State against unjust legislation by their own State." The Supreme Court consequently affirmed the trial court holding that removing the case to federal court was unwarranted.[24]

In considering Strauder's appeal the U.S. Supreme Court focused on two legal questions: First, does the Constitution of the United States afford citizens of the United States a right to trial by a jury selected and impaneled without discrimination against prospective jurors on account of a juror's race or color? Second, if such a right exists and is denied by the state, may the case be removed to federal court pursuant to Congress's power of enforcement under the Fourteenth Amendment?

Justice William Strong wrote the Opinion of the Court which held that categorical exclusion of blacks from juries for no other reason than their race violated the Equal Protection Clause. Indeed, the Court found, the very purpose of the Clause was "to assure to the colored race the enjoyment of all the civil rights that under the law are enjoyed by white persons, and to give to that race the protection of the general government,

---

[24] Klarman, Michael J. "The Racial Origins of Modern Criminal Procedure". *Mich. L. Rev.* 99: 1, 48–97 (2000).

in that enjoyment, whenever it should be denied by the States." The Court did not say that exclusion of blacks from juries violated the rights of potential jury members, but such exclusion violated the rights of black criminal defendants since juries would be "drawn from a panel from which the State has expressly excluded every man of [a defendant's] race."

However, the Court did not strike down West Virginia's law respecting juror qualifications as unconstitutional precisely because Strauder had not challenged the law as such. Instead, it proceeded with an analysis of whether the denial of equal protection of the law confronting Strauder was of a nature sufficient to motivate an exercise of Congressional authority under Section 5 of the Fourteenth Amendment to enact the law allowing for the removal of cases such as Strauder to the local federal district court, presumably where the trial process, under the supervision of a federal judge, would enforce the defendant's rights against the state.[25]

## The Scottsboro Boys

No crime in American history, before or since, has produced as many trials, convictions, reversals, and retrials as did an alleged gang rape of two white girls by nine black teenagers on a Southern Railroad freight run on March 25, 1931. The defendants were collectively known as the Scottsboro Boys and over the course of the two decades that followed, there were numerous trials and, convictions, and appeals.

Approximately two dozen young whites and black males, rode the Southern Railroad's Chattanooga to Memphis freight on March 25, 1931. Among them were four black Chattanooga teenagers hoping to investigate a rumor of government jobs in Memphis hauling logs on the river and five other black teens from various parts of Georgia. Four young whites, two males and two females dressed in overalls, also rode the train, returning to Huntsville from unsuccessful job searches in the cotton mills of Chattanooga. Soon after the train crossed the Alabama border, a white youth walked across the top of a tank car. He stepped on the hand of a black youth named Haywood Patterson, who was hanging on to its side.

---

[25] Schmidt, Benno C., Jr., "Juries, Jurisdiction, and Race Discrimination: The Lost Promise of *Strauder v. West Virginia*," *TX L. Rev.* 61: 1401 (1983).

Patterson had friends aboard the train. A fight erupted between several white youths and a larger group of black youths. Eventually, the blacks succeeded in forcing all but one of the members of the white gang off the train.

Patterson pulled the one remaining white youth, Orville Gilley, back onto the train after it had accelerated to a life-endangering speed. Some of the whites forced off the train went to the railroad authorities in Stevenson to report what they described as an assault by a gang of blacks. The station master wired ahead and a posse in Paint Rock, Alabama, stopped the train. Several white men with guns rushed at the train and the armed men rounded up every black youth they could find. Nine captured blacks were tied together with plow line, loaded on a flat back truck, and taken to a jail in Scottsboro. Nine black men were accused of raping the two young white women. Initially both women accused no less than a dozen young black men of rape. One girl also claimed the assailants were armed with guns and knives. The other woman later retracted the claims. The governor of Alabama, B. M. Miller, ordered units of the National Guard to Scottsboro to protect the suspects.

They were not told they could hire lawyers and had no access to any legal assistance until shortly before trial, leaving little or no time to plan the defense. Two attorneys eventually represented all the defendants. Stephen Moody was a real estate solicitor who was inebriated at the trial. Milo Moody was age 70 and had not tried a criminal case in decades. The two men clearly had little interest in winning acquittal. The defense lawyers demonstrated their incompetence in many ways. They were willing to try all the defendants in one lot, including one 13 year old. Defendants were tried in smaller batches only because the state feared losing on some technicality, thus freeing all defendants.

Guilty verdicts in the first trial were announced while the second trial was underway. The large crowd outside the courthouse let out a roar of approval that was clearly heard by the second jury inside. When the four trials were over, eight of the nine Scottsboro Boys had been convicted and sentenced to death. A mistrial was declared in the case of 12-year old Roy Wright, when eleven of the jurors held out for death despite the request of the prosecution for only a life sentence in view of his tender age.

The National Association for the Advancement of Colored People (NAACP) demurred. The Communist Party jumped at the opportunity to make the Scottsboro case its own. The Party saw the case as a great recruiting tool among southern blacks and northern liberals. The Communist Party, through its legal arm, the International Labor Defense (ILD), pronounced the case against the Boys a "murderous frame-up" and began efforts, ultimately successful, to be named as their attorneys. NAACP entered the picture too late despite obtaining the services of Clarence Darrow.

The ILD won its appeal to the Alabama state Supreme Court. In January, 1932, that court by a six to one vote, affirmed all but one of the eight convictions and death sentences. The court ruled that Eugene Williams, age 13, should have not been tried as an adult. The cases were appealed to the United States Supreme Court.

The defendants appealed the Alabama Supreme Court's ruling to the U.S. Supreme Court. The Supreme Court held that due process of law had been violated. Chief Justice Sutherland chose to write the opinion of the Supreme Court:[26]

> In the light of the ... ignorance and illiteracy of the defendants, their youth, the circumstances of public hostility, the imprisonment and the close surveillance of the defendants by the military forces, the fact that their friends and families were all in other states and communication with them necessarily difficult, and above all that they stood in deadly peril of their lives—we think the failure of the trial court to give them reasonable time and opportunity to secure counsel was a clear denial of due process. But passing that, and assuming their inability, even if opportunity had been given, to employ counsel, under the circumstances just stated, the necessity of counsel was so vital and imperative that the failure of the trial court to make an effective appointment of counsel was likewise a denial of due process within the meaning of the Fourteenth Amendment. .... Whether this would be

---

[26] Klarman, Michael J., "The Racial Origins of Modern Criminal Procedure". *Michigan Law Review.* 99 (1): 48–97 (2000)

so in other criminal prosecutions, or under other circumstances, we need not determine. All that it is necessary now to decide, as we do decide, is that in a capital case, where the defendant is unable to employ counsel, and is incapable adequately of making his own defense because of ignorance, feeble-mindedness, illiteracy, or the like, it is the duty of the court, whether requested or not, to assign counsel for him as a necessary requisite of due process of law; and that duty is not discharged by an assignment at such a time or under such circumstances as to preclude the giving of effective aid in the preparation and trial of the case. . . . necessary, is a logical corollary from the constitutional right to be heard by counsel.[27]

For the retrial the ILD selected two attorneys to represent the Scottsboro Boys. The ILD secured the services of Samuel Leibowitz to serve as the lead defense attorney. Leibowitz was a New York criminal attorney who had secured an astonishing record of seventy-seven acquittals and one hung jury in seventy-eight murder trials. Leibowitz was a mainline Democrat with no connections with or sympathies toward the Communist Party. Joseph Brodsky, the ILD's chief attorney, was selected to assist Leibowitz. The subsequent trials produced conflicting testimony, retraction of the rape charge by one alleged victim, antisemitism directed against Leibowitz, prejudice by the trial judges, and multiple errors. While the defendants were found guilty once again the defense appealed to the U.S. Supreme Court and won once again.

On February 15, 1935, the United States Supreme Court heard arguments in the Patterson and Norris cases. Leibowitz argued that the convictions should be overturned because Alabama excluded blacks from its jury rolls in violation of the equal protection clause of the Constitution. The names of blacks that appeared on the jury rolls introduced in Judge Callahan's courtroom were, Leibowitz told the justices, forged sometime after the start of Patterson's trial. Chief Justice Charles Evans Hughes asked Leibowitz if he could prove that allegation. Leibowitz had a page bring in the actual jury rolls and a magnifying glass. Hughes looked at the

---

[27] *Powell v. Alabama*, 287 U.S. 45 (1932)

rolls, then passed it to the next seated justice, who then passed it to the next. Looks of disgust appeared on their faces. Six weeks later the Supreme Court announced their decision in *Norris vs. Alabama*, unanimously holding that the Alabama system of jury selection unconstitutional and reversing the convictions of Norris and Patterson. Leibowitz said, "I am thrilled beyond words." He hoped that the Court's decision would convince Alabama that the Scottsboro cases were no longer worth their economic and political cost.[28]

As the state prepared for a fourth trial of the Scottsboro Boys two ILD lawyers in Nashville were arrested and charged with trying to bribe Victoria Price to change her testimony, infuriating Leibowitz, who said the ILD was "assassinating" the Scottsboro Boys. Meanwhile, Leibowitz, meanwhile, was charged with alienating potential jurors so Leibowitz agreed to let a local attorney named Charles Watts play the more visible role while he coached from a seat behind. Defendant was again convicted of rape, but the jury sentenced him to seventy-five years in prison rather than giving him the death sentence. The verdict represented the first time in the history of Alabama that a black man convicted of raping a white woman had not been sentenced to death.

Seven of the nine Scottsboro Boys had been held in jail for over six years without trial by the time jury selection began in the third trial of Clarence Norris on Monday, July 12, 1937. The new prosecutor announced that the state was dropping rape charges against Powell and that he was pleading guilty to assaulting a deputy. Then all charges were dropped against the remaining four defendants: Willie Roberson, Olen Montgomery, Eugene Williams, and Roy Wright. Wright and Williams were 12 and 13 at the time of the incident and, in view of the jail time they had already served, justice required that they also be released.

In 1938, it appeared that Governor Bibb Graves was anxious to end the episode and that the five would be released after he had his traditional pre-pardon interviews with each in his office. The interviews went badly and none of the incarcerated defendants admitted any knowledge or guilt concerning a rape. Graves left office without issuing

---

[28] *Norris v. Alabama*, 294 U.S. 587 (1935).

the pardons. Either through paroles or escapes all of the Scottsboro Boys eventually found their way out of Alabama.[29]

Because of its principled leadership in the Scottsboro campaign, the Communist Party gained much widespread respect among blacks and civil rights activists of all colors. When they traveled to Washington, D.C. to demonstrate, the Communist Party stopped at segregated restaurants to stage sit-ins against discrimination, helping to turn the campaign into a trial of the system of segregation and racism in America, showing its next campaign.

## *Swain v. Alabama*

Swain was a black man who was indicted and convicted of rape in the Circuit Court of Talladega County, Alabama, and sentenced to death. Of those in the county eligible for jury selection for grand and petit juries, 26% were blacks. However, the jury panels between 1953 and 1964 averaged 10% to 15% blacks. In the case at hand, there were four or five blacks on the grand jury panel, and two blacks had served on the grand jury. Although petit jury venires in criminal cases included an average of six to seven blacks, none had served on any petit jury in the county since about 1950. In the case of Swain, of the eight blacks on the venire, two were exempt, and six were peremptorily struck by the prosecutor. The Alabama Supreme Court rejected the petitioner's motions to quash the indictment, to strike the trial jury venire, and to void the trial jury, all based on discrimination in the selection of jurors.[30]

In a 6-3 decision, the Supreme Court affirmed the decision of the Alabama Supreme Court, holding that neither the racial disparity in jury pools nor the decade-long absence of any black juror to serve at trial presented evidence sufficient to "make out a prima facie case of invidious discrimination under the Fourteenth Amendment." This case recognized the peremptory challenge as a valid legal practice so long as it was not

---

[29] Carter, Dan T., *Scottsboro: A Tragedy of the American South*, revised ed. (Baton Rouge: Louisiana State University Press, 1979); Philip S. Foner and Herbert Shapiro, eds., *American Communism and Black Americans: A Documentary History, 1930–1934* (Philadelphia: Temple University Press, 1991).

[30] *Swain v. Alabama*, 380 U.S. 202 (1965)

used intentionally to exclude blacks from jury duties.

The U.S. Supreme Court held that a defendant in a criminal case is not constitutionally entitled to a proportionate number of his race on the trial jury or the jury panel. Justice Byron White authored the Opinion of the Court. Swain had not shown "purposeful racial discrimination." by showing only that one identifiable group had been underrepresented by as much as 10%. The high court found no evidence in this case that the jury commissioners had applied different jury selection standards as between blacks and whites. Moreover, an imperfect system of selection of jury panels is not the equivalent of purposeful racial discrimination. The court also found that the prosecutor's striking of Negroes from the jury panel in one particular case under the peremptory challenge system, which permits a challenge without a reason stated, does not constitute denial of equal protection of the laws. Moreover, even if a State's systematic striking of blacks in selecting trial juries raises a prima facie case of discrimination under the Fourteenth Amendment, the defendant had presented no record in his case that was sufficient to establish such a systematic striking in the county. Bottom line is that the petitioner had the burden of proof, and he had failed to meet it. It is true that the total exclusion of blacks from venires by state officials creates an inference of discrimination, but this rule of proof cannot be applied where it is not shown that the state is responsible for the exclusion of Negroes through peremptory challenges.[31]

Justice Goldberg authored a dissent which was joined by Justice Douglas and Chief Justice Warren. The dissent factored in the later case *Batson v. Kentucky*[32] which overturned *Swain*.

## *Batson v. Kentucky*

James Kirkland Batson was a black man convicted of burglary and receipt of stolen goods in a Louisville, Kentucky. The circuit court had a jury composed entirely of white persons. Batson's appeal was based on the jury selection, or *voir dire*, phase of the trial. During this phase potential jurors are examined by the Court, the prosecution, and the defense, to determine their competence, willingness, and suitability to hear, deliberate

[31] 380 U. S. 226-227; 275 Ala. 508, 156 So.2d 368, affirmed.
[32] *Batson v. Kentucky*, 476 U.S. 79 (1986)

and decide a case put to them to render a just and fair verdict. During *voir dire* the judge can dismiss jurors and both the prosecution and the defense have a limited number of peremptory challenges, which are accepted as the right of the party making the challenge and which they use to excuse any juror for any reason which the particular side believes will help their case.

In Batson's case, the judge dismissed several potential jurors for various causes. The defense peremptorily challenged nine potential jurors and the prosecutor, Joe Gutmann, peremptorily challenged six, including all four black persons. Thus, a jury composed only of white persons was selected. The defense counsel moved to discharge the whole jury on the ground that the prosecutor's removal of all black veniremen violated petitioner's rights under the Sixth and Fourteenth Amendments to a jury drawn from a cross section of the community, and under the Fourteenth Amendment to equal protection of the laws. Without expressly ruling on petitioner's request for a hearing, the trial judge denied the motion, and the jury subsequently convicted the defendant.

The defendant appealed his conviction to the Kentucky Supreme Court, which affirmed the conviction, citing *Swain v. Alabama.* That case had held that a defendant alleging lack of a fair cross section must demonstrate systematic exclusion of a group of jurors from the panel of prospective jurors. That is, the defendant had to show that not just in his case, but as a process, juries in his community were being constructed so as to not represent a cross section of that community. Batson continued his appeal to the U.S. Supreme Court, which granted certiorari to decide whether petitioner was tried "in violation of constitutional provisions guaranteeing the defendant an impartial jury and a jury composed of persons representing a fair cross section of the community.

Justice Powell wrote the decision of the Supreme Court. In a 7–2 decision, the Court held that, while a defendant is not entitled to have a jury completely or partially composed of people of his own race, the state is not permitted to use its peremptory challenges to automatically exclude potential members of the jury because of their race. "The Equal Protection Clause guarantees the defendant that the state will not exclude members of his race from the jury venire on account of race or on the false assumption that members of his race as a group are not qualified to serve as jurors." Justice Powell continued, "The harm from discriminatory jury selection extends beyond that inflicted on the defendant and the excluded juror to touch the entire community. Selection procedures that purposefully exclude black persons from juries undermine public confidence in the fairness of our system of justice."

Thus, a defendant in a criminal case can make an Equal Protection claim based on the discriminatory use of peremptory challenges at a defendant's trial. Once the defendant makes a showing that race was the reason potential jurors were excluded, the burden shifts to the state to come forward with a race-neutral explanation for the exclusion.

In concurrence Justice White wrote that although the Court's prior precedent should have warned prosecutors that using peremptory challenges to exclude people based solely on race violates the Equal Protection Clause, the widespread practice of discriminatory elimination of jurors justifies the opportunity to inquire into the basis of the peremptory challenge.[33]

In dissent Justice Thurgood Marshall wrote in *Batson* that discrimination would end only with the elimination of peremptory strikes. These arbitrary removals of potential jurors often disguised racial prejudices.

In the State of Washington in 2013 Kirk Saintcalle, a black man, challenged his conviction for first degree felony murder because the prosecution had used a peremptory challenge to strike the only black venireperson in his jury pool. Saintcalle claimed the peremptory strike was clearly racially motivated in violation of the equal protection guaranty discovered in *Batson v. Kentucky*.[34] The Washington State Supreme Court disagreed because *Batson* requires a finding of purposeful discrimination, and the trial court's finding that there was no purposeful discrimination here. Accordingly, it affirmed Saintcalle's conviction. The court's comments that followed are interesting:

However, we also take this opportunity to examine

---

[33] *Batson v. Kentucky* 476 U.S. 79 (1986)
[34] 476 U.S. 79, 106 S. Ct. 1712, 90 L. Ed. 2d 69 (1986)

whether our Batson procedures are robust enough to effectively combat race discrimination in the selection of juries. We conclude that they are not. Twenty-six years after Batson, a growing body of evidence shows that racial discrimination remains rampant in jury selection. In part, this is because Batson recognizes only "purposeful discrimination," whereas racism is often unintentional, institutional, or unconscious. We conclude that our Batson procedures must change and that we must strengthen Batson to recognize these more prevalent forms of discrimination. But we will not create a new standard in this case because the issue has not been raised, briefed, or argued, and indeed, the parties are not seeking to advance a new standard. Applying Batson, we affirm the Court of Appeals.[35]

## *McCleskey v. Kemp*

McCleskey, a black man, was convicted in a Georgia trial court of armed robbery and murder, arising from the killing of a white police officer during the robbery of a store. The jury at the penalty hearing considered the various mitigating and aggravating circumstances, and recommended the death penalty on the murder charge. The Georgia Supreme Court affirmed. After unsuccessfully seeking post-conviction relief in state courts, petitioner sought *habeas corpus* relief in Federal District Court.

In his petition to the U.S. Supreme Court, McCleskey claimed that the capital sentencing process in Georgia was administered in a racially discriminatory manner in violation of the Eighth and Fourteenth Amendments. In support of the claim, petitioner proffered the Baldus statistical study that claimed to show a disparity in the imposition of the death sentence in Georgia based on the murder victim's race and, to a lesser extent, the defendant's race. The Baldus study was based on over 2,000 murder cases that occurred in Georgia during the 1970's, and involved data relating to the victim's race, the defendant's race, and the various combinations of such persons' races. The study concluded that

---

[35] *State of Washington v. Kirk Ricardo Saintcalle* (2013). 86257-5

black defendants who killed white victims have the greatest likelihood of receiving the death penalty. Rejecting petitioner's constitutional claims, the Federal District Court denied his petition insofar as it was based on the Baldus study. The Court of Appeals affirmed the District Court's decision on this issue. While it accepted the validity of the Baldus study, it found that the statistics were insufficient to demonstrate unconstitutional discrimination in the Fourteenth Amendment context or to show irrationality, arbitrariness, and capriciousness under Eighth Amendment analysis. The case moved to the U.S. Supreme Court where it was argued on 15 October 1986.

Justice Powell delivered the Opinion of the Court. In it he was joined by Justices Rehnquist, White, O'Connor, and Scalia. The opinion held that Baldus study did not prove that the administration of the Georgia capital punishment system violates the Equal Protection Clause. In order to prevail under that Clause, McCleskey had to prove that the decision makers in his case acted with discriminatory purpose to which the petitioner offered no evidence specific proof relative to his own case. McCleskey failed to show that racial considerations played a part in his sentence. The Baldus study alone was insufficient to support an inference that anyone in his case acted with discriminatory purpose. This Court has accepted statistics as proof of intent to discriminate in the context of a State's selection.

The court held that there was no merit to petitioner's argument that the Baldus study proved that the State has violated the Equal Protection Clause by adopting the capital punishment statute and allowing it to remain in force despite its allegedly discriminatory application. In order for this claim to prevail, McCleskey would have to prove that the Georgia legislature enacted or maintained the death penalty statute because of an anticipated racially discriminatory effect. There simply was no evidence that the legislature either enacted the statute to further a racially discriminatory purpose.

Justice Powell wrote that there was no merit to the contention that the Baldus study showed that Georgia's capital punishment system is arbitrary and capricious in application. The statistics do not prove that race enters into any capital sentencing decisions or that race was a factor in petitioner's case. The likelihood of racial prejudice allegedly shown by the study does not constitute the constitutional measure of an unacceptable risk of racial prejudice. The inherent lack of predictability of jury decisions does not justify their condemnation. On the contrary, it is the jury's function to make the difficult and uniquely human judgments that defy codification and that build discretion, equity, and flexibility into the legal system. At the most, the Baldus study indicates a discrepancy that appears to correlate with race, but this discrepancy does not constitute a major systemic defect. Any mode for determining guilt or punishment has its weaknesses and the potential for misuse. Despite such imperfections, constitutional guarantees are met when the mode for determining guilt or punishment has been surrounded with safeguards to make it as fair as possible. The Constitution does not require that a State eliminate any demonstrable disparity that correlates with a potentially irrelevant factor in order to operate a criminal justice system that includes capital punishment. Petitioner's arguments are best presented to the legislative bodies, not the courts.

Justice Blackmun filed a dissenting opinion in which Justices Marshall and Stevens in part or in whole.[36]

# North Carolina Racial Justice Act

Under the Racial Justice Act (RJA) in North Carolina, a capital defendant can have his or her sentence reduced to life in prison without parole if there is evidence proving "that race was a significant factor in decisions to seek or impose the sentence of death in the county, the prosecurial district, the judicial division, or the State at the time the death sentence was sought or imposed." Defendants may present evidence in any of three categories: first, evidence that death sentences were sought or imposed more frequently upon defendants of one race than others; second evidence that death sentences were sought or imposed more frequently on behalf of victims of one race than others, or, third, evidence that race was a significant factor in decisions to exercise peremptory strikes during jury selection. Any one of these three categories is

---

[36] *McCleskey v. Kemp*, 481 U.S. 279 (1987)

sufficient to establish a RJA violation.[37]

The North Carolina repealed the Legislature Racial Justice Act in 2013. In the first case to advance to an evidentiary hearing under the RJA, *Robinson* introduced a wealth of evidence showing the persistent, pervasive, and distorting role of race in jury selection throughout North Carolina. The evidence, largely unrebutted by the State, requires relief in his case and should serve as a clear signal of the need for reform in capital jury selection proceedings in the future. In December 2015, the North Carolina Supreme Court vacated the decisions in the case of *North Carolina v. Robinson* and three subsequent cases in which defendants' death sentences had been reduced to life, holding that the state had not been given sufficient time to review and respond to the studies on racial bias in jury selection. *Robinson* presented evidence in the third category, peremptory strikes during jury selection. Peremptory strikes allow prosecutors and defense lawyers to remove members of the jury pool they believe may be unfavorable to their side, provided they may not target venire members based on race or gender. In fact, the North Carolina Conference of District Attorneys had presented a statewide training course in 1995 that included a handout called *Batson Justifications: Articulating Juror Negatives*, listing 10 modes of justifications that can be offered as racially-neutral explanations for the exclusion of potential jurors.[38]

In 1994, Marcus Robinson, a young Black man, was convicted of killing Erik Tornblom, a young white man. Robinson had just turned 18 some 80 days before the crime. Had he committed the murder less than three months earlier he would have been ineligible for the death penalty.

In the first ruling under North Carolina's Racial Justice Act Superior Court Judge Gregory Weeks altered the sentence in *Robinson*. Judge Weeks held that evidence of intentional discrimination is not required. "To hold that a defendant cannot prevail under the RJA unless he

---

[37] N. C. Gen. Stat. §15A-2010

[38] Pollitt, Daniel R. and Warren, Brittany P., "Thirty Years of Disappointment: North Carolina's Remarkable Appellate *Batson* Record", 94 *N.C. L. Rev.* 1957 (2016); Grosso, Catherine and O'Brien, Barbara, "A Stubborn Legacy: The Overwhelming Importance of Race in Jury Selection in 173 Post-*Batson* North Carolina Capital Trials," 97 *Iowa L. Rev.* 1531 (2012)

proves intentional discrimination would read a requirement into the statute that the General Assembly clearly did not place there." In addition, the defendant does not have to prove discrimination in his or her particular case because the General Assembly excluded such a provision from the final version of the RJA. He continued, ""In enacting RJA, the North Carolina General Assembly made clear that the law of North Carolina rejects the influence of race discrimination in the administration of the death penalty. The RJA represents a landmark reform in North Carolina, a state which has long been a leader in forward-thinking criminal justice policies." In recognizing the use of peremptory strikes to remove black jurors, Judge Weeks wrote, "Discrimination in jury selection frustrates the commitment of African-Americans to full participation in civic life. One of the stereotypes particularly offensive to African-American citizens is that they are not interested in seeing criminals brought to justice. African-Americans who have been excluded from jury service on account of race compare their experiences to the injustice and humiliations of the Jim Crow era."[39]

In December 2015, the North Carolina Supreme Court vacated the decisions in *North Carolina v. Robinson* and three subsequent cases in which defendants' death sentences had been reduced to life, holding that the state had not been given sufficient time to review and respond to the studies on racial bias in jury selection. On remand, rather than hold a new hearing with more time for the State's case, the new trial court simply dismissed Robinson's case entirely. Robinson has asked the state high court to grant review because this dismissal violates a host of constitutional protections and state laws, including those prohibiting racial discrimination in capital cases.[40]

## *Flowers v. Mississippi*

The U.S. Supreme Court has agreed to review whether a prosecutor with a long history of racially discriminatory jury-selection practices unconstitutionally struck black jurors in the trial of Mississippi

---

[39] Ruling of Superior Court, Judge Gregory Weeks, *North Carolina v. Robinson*, April 22, 2012

[40] https://deathpenaltyinfo.org/north-carolina-racial-justice-act-ruling-summary

death-row prisoner Curtis Giovanni Flowers. On November 2, 2018, the Court granted certiorari in the Flowers's case on the question of "[w]hether the Mississippi Supreme Court erred in how it applied *Batson v. Kentucky*," the landmark 1986 Supreme Court decision barring the use of discretionary strikes to remove jurors on the basis of race.

Flowers has been tried six times for a notorious 1996 quadruple murder in Winona, Mississippi. He was prosecuted each time by Doug Evans, the District Attorney in Mississippi's Fifth Circuit Court District since 1992. All-white or nearly all-white juries convicted Flowers based on questionable circumstantial evidence which has subsequently been challenged and also on the testimony of a jailhouse informant. The informant has subsequently recanted his testimony that Flowers had confessed to the murders. Court pleadings and neutral examinations have cast doubt upon much of the evidence in the case. One prominent pathologist who examined the autopsy reports and crime scene photograph disputed the prosecution's theory that the murder was committed by a single perpetrator.

A recent study of jury selection in the Fifth Circuit Court District during the 26-year period from 1992 to 2017 in which Evans was District Attorney, analyzed prosecurial strikes or acceptances of more than 6,700 jurors in the 225 trials conducted. Throughout his tenure Evans struck prospective black jurors at nearly 4½ times the rate of white prospective jurors. In the case of Curtis Flowers, Evans struck nearly all of the black jurors in each trial. In his first three trials, the Mississippi Supreme Court overturned Flowers's convictions because of prosecurial misconduct, with courts finding that Evans had violated the *Batson* rule in two of those trials. The fourth and fifth trials ended in mistrials. In the sixth trial, in June 2010, Evans accepted the first qualified potential black juror and then struck the remaining five in the jury pool. Flowers challenged the prosecution's jury strikes on appeal, but the Mississippi Supreme Court, over the dissents of three justices, rejected his claim.

In June 2016, the United States Supreme Court vacated the state court's ruling and returned the case to the Mississippi Supreme Court to reconsider the issue in light of the Court's decision one month earlier in *Foster v. Chatman*, finding that prosecutors in a Georgia capital case had unconstitutionally stricken jurors because they were black. However, over the dissents of three justices, the Mississippi Supreme Court again affirmed, writing that the prior adjudications that Evans had already twice violated *Batson* "do not undermine Evans' race neutral reasons" for striking black jurors in the sixth trial and that "the historical evidence of past discrimination ... does not alter our analysis."[41]

## *Foster v. Chatman*

In 1986 Timothy Foster, a black 18-year-old male, was accused of killing Queen Madge White, a 79-year-old white woman and retired schoolteacher in Georgia. She had been sexually assaulted and murdered in her home, which was ransacked. A month later, law enforcement officers were called to a domestic disturbance at the home of one Lisa Stubbs. She told the officers that her boyfriend, Timothy Foster, had killed White. He also had gifted items stolen from White's house to her and to various family members. Police arrested Foster who admitted to the crime. Police recovered some of the stolen items from White's house at the Foster residence. Foster was convicted of capital murder and sentenced to death in a Georgia court.

During jury selection at his trial, the State used peremptory challenges to strike all four black prospective jurors qualified to serve on the jury. Foster argued that the prosecution had used those strikes to racially manipulate the jury in violation of constitutional requirements.[42] The trial court rejected that claim, and the Georgia Supreme Court affirmed the decision.

Foster then renewed his Batson claim in a state *habeas corpus* proceeding. Foster, through the Georgia Open Records Act, obtained from the State copies of the file used by the prosecution during his trial. Among other documents, the file contained copies of the jury venire list on which the names of each black prospective juror were highlighted in bright green, with a legend indicating that the highlighting "represents Blacks"; a draft

---

[41] *Flowers v. Mississippi.* Motion to proceed in forma pauperis and petition for a writ of certiorari granted, judgment vacated and case remanded for further consideration in light of *Foster v. Chatman* on June 20, 2016.

[42] *Batson v. Kentucky*, 476 U. S. 79

affidavit from an investigator comparing black prospective jurors and concluding, "If it comes down to having to pick one of the black jurors, [this one] might be okay"; notes identifying black prospective jurors as "B#1," "B#2," and "B#3"; notes with "N" (for "no") appearing next to the names of all black prospective jurors; a list titled "[D]efinite NO's" containing six names, including the names of all of the qualified black prospective jurors; a document with notes on the Church of Christ that was annotated "No. No Black Church"; and finally the questionnaires filled out by five prospective black jurors, on which each juror's response indicating his or her race had been circled.

The state *habeas court* did not grant relief. It noted that Foster's Batson claim had been adjudicated on direct appeal. Because Foster's renewed *Batson* claim did not demonstrate purposeful discrimination," the court concluded that he had failed to show "any change in the facts sufficient to overcome" the state law doctrine of res judicata. The Georgia Supreme Court denied Foster the Certificate of Probable Cause necessary to file an appeal.

On 23 May 2016, the U.S. Supreme Court ruled in *Foster v. Chatman* ruled that Timothy Foster had indeed established purposeful racial discrimination by the prosecution's dismissal of two black jurors during jury selection at his trial, in violation of the *Batson* rule. After dealing with a minor procedural issue, the Court decided that Foster established purposeful racial discrimination in the prosecution's dismissal of two black jurors: Marilyn Garrett and Eddie Hood. By a vote of 7-1, the Court determined that Foster, armed with his newly discovered evidence of purposeful racial discrimination, was eligible to have his *Batson* claim reevaluated.

The Supreme Court's decision could pave the way for numerous other similarly situated capital defendants to have their own decades-old *Batson* claims reevaluated based on newly discovered evidence of purposeful racial discrimination.[43]

---

[43] *Foster v Chatman,* 578 U.S. --- (2016); Docket 14-8349

## Another Type of Discrimination

Thirteen year-old Mary Phagan had worked at Atlanta's National Pencil Company factory since she was just 12-years old. On the afternoon of Saturday, April 26th, 1913, Mary dropped into her workplace to pick up her meager wages for the week, hoping to then attend that day's Confederate Memorial Day parade in the town center. The factory's manager was Leo Frank, a 29-year-old graduate of Cornell University whose wealthy uncle who owned multiple shares in the factory's parent company had secured the position for him. At about noon Mary made her way to his office to collect her meager wage, an encounter Frank recalled later when interviewed by the police. He would be the last person to admit to seeing the teenager alive.

The next morning, the factory's night-watchman Newt Lee made a horrific discovery. In the basement of the building he found the battered and bloodied body of a young girl. Mary Phagan had been beaten, raped and strangled with a cord cut deep into her neck. Lee immediately summoned the local police. He was arrested and charged with the crime by police, the next day a white mob gathering outside of the station with the intent of lynching him. Newt Lee was saved from the mob and later cleared of any involvement.

Police then began interviewing current and former workers at the factory. On May first detectives called around at the house of factory superintendent Leo Frank. Although not detained at this time, the officers were extremely suspicious of Frank. From the tentative timeline they had assembled of Mary Phagan's day, Frank was the last person to admit to having seen her alive.

A coroners jury re-examined the factory crime scene and found blond hairs and blood in the metal room near to Frank's office. Another young factory girl also testified that she had come to collect her wage shortly after Mary but Frank was not in his office. On the basis of this evidence, and his nervy demeanor, Frank was arrested on suspicion of the murder. Another man, the factory's black janitor Jim Conley, was also arrested after witnesses saw him washing red stains out of a shirt in a faucet behind the factory. Whilst Conley gave numerous contradictory statements

about the murder, he would later be used as the chief witness against Leo
Frank at the trial. Leo Frank became their prime suspect. Conley
eventually testified that Frank had killed Phagan and he had helped him
dispose of the body. Both the coroners jury and the grand jury unanimously
voted to indict Frank for the murder.

The trial began on July 28th 1913, with state attorney Hugh
Dorsey leading the prosecution. Dorsey attempted to portray the defendant
as a sexual predator and pervert, producing a succession of young women
from the pencil factory to testify that Frank had made improper advances
to them. Conley's testimony was enough to convince the jury and Frank
was unanimously convicted. On October 10th, Judge Leonard S. Roan
sentenced Leo Frank to hang.[44]

Prominent Jewish organizations, businessmen and media tycoons
rallied behind Frank's innocence and campaigned to overturn the guilty
verdict. Numerous stories appeared in the press which sided with Frank
and tried to cast the spotlight of blame on alternative, black, suspects.

Much of the press coverage both against and in favor of Frank was
shockingly racist by today's standards, but about what was to be expected
for the course for the American South in 1913. Specifically, much
coverage alleging Frank's innocence was highly inflammatory anti-black
in nature since it alleged that a black man not Frank had killed and raped
Mary Phagan. In a society built around discrimination, the sad murder of
Mary Phagan thus became polarized between two camps of differing but
equally extreme prejudices.

Frank's family made numerous appeals, including an appeal to the
Supreme Court of the United States, all of which failed. Governor John M.
Slaton commuted Frank's sentence from capital punishment to life
imprisonment, effectively ending his own public career. On August 16,
1915, Frank was kidnapped from his prison cell and lynched at Marietta,
Mary Phagan's hometown, the next morning. The new governor vowed to
punish the lynchers, who included prominent Marietta citizens, but
nobody was charged.

---

[44] *Atlanta Journal*, 25 August 1913.

For those advocating Frank's innocence, he was the victim of the antisemitism endemic in American society; in its police and judiciary. For this camp, the true culprit was obviously the violent black man, unable to control his urge to ravage an innocent white girl.

Those who believed Frank had murdered Mary painted his supporters as part of an insidious Jewish conspiracy to help one of their own escape justice, tapping into the wider and more sinister beliefs of the time that a Jewish cabal of industrialists and bankers was taking over America.

In 1937, Mervyn LeRoy directed the movie *They Won't Forget,* based on the Ward Greene novel *Death in The Deep South,* which was in turn inspired by the Frank case. These works suggested that the prosecuting attorney thought he would have an easy case against the probable murderer, Jim Conley, but he could advance his career by prosecuting Frank, Northern Jew.[45] Later television docudramas looked at the trial. One made for television movie awarded Governor Slaton a place among American profiles in courage for his action.

Among other results was the rise of the Ku Klux Klan and a consequent wave of anti-Jewish literature and behavior. All this worked to delay the placement of blacks on Southern juries.

---

[45] There is an excellent account of the Murder of Mary Phagan on Wikipedia. See also Scholnick, Myron L., *Journal of Southern History,* Vol. 61, No. 4 (November 1995), pp. 860–861; Alphin, Elaine Marie. *An Unspeakable Crime: The Prosecution and Persecution of Leo Frank.* Carolrhoda Books, 2010; and Carter, Dan. "And the Dead Shall Rise: The Murder of Mary Phagan and the Lynching of Leo Frank". *Journal of Southern History*, Vol. 71, Issue 2 (May 2005).

# Abandonment and Reinstatement of the Death Penalty

Despite its long history of application and imposition the death penalty has come under intensive examination by the political left. Activists of the liberal persuasion once in control of the U.S. Supreme Court added the abolition of capital punishment to its social agenda. When conservatives have been in a majority on recent high courts the decisions have been more favorable to its retention. Liberals can easily claim substantial victory because of the whittling down of the number and type of cases where capital punishment can be imposed. Probably the most effective tool in the arsenal of the opponents of capital punishment has been the race card for it was true that death sentences were far more likely to be imposed on black criminals than white one for the same acts in similar situations.

## *Witherspoon v. Illinois*

The petitioner, William C. Witherspoon, was brought to trial in 1960 in Cook County, Illinois, on a charge of murder. The jury found him guilty and fixed his penalty at death. At the time of his trial an Illinois statute provided: "In trials for murder it shall be a cause for challenge of any juror who shall, on being examined, state that he has conscientious scruples against capital punishment, or that he is opposed to the same." Through this provision the State of Illinois armed the prosecution with unlimited challenges for cause in order to exclude those jurors who, in the words of the State's highest court, "might hesitate to return a verdict inflicting [death]." At the petitioner's trial, the prosecution eliminated nearly half the venire of prospective jurors by challenging, under the authority of this statute, any venireman who expressed qualms about capital punishment. The trial judge early on decided to remove conscientious objectors, "without wasting any time on them." In rapid succession, 47 veniremen were successfully challenged for cause on the basis of their attitudes toward the death penalty, although only five of the 47 explicitly stated that under no circumstances would they vote to impose capital punishment. From those who remained were chosen the jurors who ultimately found the petitioner guilty and sentenced him to death. The Supreme Court had to decide whether the Constitution permits a State to execute a man pursuant to the verdict of a jury so composed.

The high court found that the petitioner failed to prove that this jury was biased with respect to the petitioner's guilt. However, it is self-evident that, in its role as arbiter of the punishment to be imposed, this jury fell woefully short of that impartiality to which the petitioner was entitled under the Sixth and Fourteenth Amendments.

Writing for the court, in his opinion Justice Stewart said, "Whatever else might be said of capital punishment, it is at least clear that its imposition by a hanging jury cannot be squared with the Constitution. The State of Illinois has stacked the deck against the petitioner. To execute this death sentence would deprive him of his life without due process of law."[46]

## McGautha v. California

*McGautha* was a criminal case heard by the United States Supreme Court, in which the Court held that the lack of legal standards by which juries imposed the death penalty was not an unconstitutional violation of the due process clause portion of the Eighth Amendment. Justice Harlan wrote that preparing rules for juries to decide the imposition of the death penalty demanded more of the state than was realistically possible. The high court was asked to view the race card, deciding whether there was unequal application of the death penalty involving blacks who killed whites. Plaintiffs alleged that Black defendants so charged were

---

[46] *Witherspoon v. Illinois*, 391 U.S. 510 (1968)

much more likely to have a death penalty imposed. The court held

> In light of history, experience, and the limitations of human knowledge in establishing definitive standards, it is impossible to say that leaving to the untrammeled discretion of the jury the power to pronounce life or death in capital cases violates any provision of the Constitution . . . . The Constitution does not prohibit the States from considering that the compassionate purposes of jury sentencing in capital cases are better served by having the issues of guilt and punishment resolved in a single trial than by focusing the jury's attention solely on punishment after guilt has been determined.[47]

## *Furman v. Georgia*

*McGautha* was overruled one year later by *Furman v. Georgia.* Direct and complete abolition of capital punishment seemed to be the result of *Furman v Georgia.* What it certainly did accomplish was a full scale moratorium for almost five years while the troops on each side gathered and perfected their best arguments.

While robbing a home, the owner of the home was awakened by the William Henry Furman who was committing a burglary. On hearing the homeowner, Furman fled the house. However, in the midst of his attempt to escape, a firearm that he had been carrying has discharged striking and killing the owner of the home. Furman claimed that the weapon discharged in an accidental fashion. He said that while trying to escape, he tripped and the weapon he was carrying fired accidentally, killing the victim. This contradicted his prior statement to police that he had turned and blindly fired a shot while fleeing. In either event, because the shooting occurred during the commission of a felony, Furman would have been guilty of murder and eligible for the death penalty under then-extant state law, according to the felony murder rule.

On review of the case details, Georgia's court explained that due to the fact that the murder took place in the midst of the commitment of a

---

[47] *McGautha v. California*, 402 U.S. 183 (1971). McGautha was heard along with *Crampton v. Ohio*, on *certiorari* to the Supreme Court of Ohio.

felony, Furman could be executed in the event of a guilty verdict. Furman appealed his execution explaining that the nature of sentencing for capital punishment lacked uniformity.[48] Capital Punishment could be imposed on convicted criminals when the presiding jury decides the death penalty to be fair and applicable punishment.

The high court issued a highly divided 5–4 decision. The Court's one-paragraph *per curium* opinion[49] held that the imposition of the death penalty in these cases constituted cruel and unusual punishment and violated the Constitution. However, the majority could not agree as to a rationale. There was no opinion of the court or plurality as none of the five justices constituting the majority joined in the opinion of any other. Justices Potter Stewart, Byron White and William O. Douglas expressed similar concerns about the apparent arbitrariness with which death sentences were imposed under the existing laws, often indicating a racial bias against black defendants. Because these opinions were the narrowest, finding only that the death penalty as currently applied was cruel and unusual, they are often considered the controlling majority opinions. Justices William Brennan and Thurgood Marshall concluded that the death penalty was in itself "cruel and unusual punishment," and incompatible with the evolving standards of decency of a contemporary society. Justice Stewart wrote:

> These death sentences are cruel and unusual in the same way that being struck by lightning is cruel and unusual. For, of all the people convicted of rapes and murders in 1967 and 1968, many just as reprehensible as these, the petitioners are among a capriciously selected random handful upon whom the sentence of death has in fact been imposed. My concurring Brothers have demonstrated that. If any basis can be discerned for the selection of these few to be sentenced to death, it is the constitutionally

---

[48] *Furman v. Georgia,* 408 U.S. 238 (1972)
[49] Latin for "by the court." An opinion from an appellate court that does not identify any specific judge who may have written the opinion. Overview. A *per curiam* decision is a court opinion issued in the name of the Court rather than specific judges. Most decisions on the merits by the courts take the form of one or more opinions written and signed by individual justices.

impermissible basis of race.[50] But racial discrimination has not been proved, and I put it to one side. I simply conclude that the Eighth and Fourteenth Amendments cannot tolerate the infliction of a sentence of death under legal systems that permit this unique penalty to be so wantonly and so freakishly imposed.

Chief Justice Warren Burger and Justices Harry Blackmun, Lewis F. Powell, and William H. Rehnquist dissented. They argued that a punishment provided in 40 state statutes and by the federal government could not be ruled contrary to the so-called "evolving standard of decency."

The Supreme Court overturned Furman's execution, stating that unless a uniform and unwavering policy of determination for the eligibility to undergo capital punishment exists, the death penalty is to be considered as 'cruel and unusual' punishment; as a result of this finding, the death penalty was deemed to be illegal within the United States.[51]

This case led to a *de facto* moratorium on capital punishment throughout the United States. The decision forced states and the U.S. Congress to reconsider their statutes for capital offenses to ensure that the death penalty would not be administered in a capricious or discriminatory manner. In the following four years, thirty-seven states enacted new death penalty laws aimed responding to the concerns about the arbitrary imposition of the death penalty. Several statutes that mandated bifurcated trials, with separate guilt-innocence and sentencing phases, and imposing standards to guide the discretion of juries and judges in imposing capital sentences. Finally state death sentence were upheld in a series of Supreme Court decisions in 1976, most importantly *Gregg v. Georgia*.[52]

## *Gregg v. Georgia*

Following *Furman,* various states amended their laws dealing with capital punishment. The states of Georgia, Florida, Texas, North

---

[50] See *McLaughlin v. Florida,* 379 U.S. 184 (1964)

[51] Henson, Burt M., and Ross R. Olney. *Furman v. Georgia: The Death Penalty and the Constitution.* New York: Franklin Watts, 1996; and Herda, D.J. *Furman v. Georgia: The Death Penalty Case.* Enslow Publishers, 1994.

[52] *Gregg v. Georgia, Proffitt v. Florida, Jurek v. Texas, Woodson v. North Carolina, and Roberts v. Louisiana,* 428 U.S. 153 (1976)

Carolina, and Louisiana had amended their death penalty statutes sufficiently to meet the *Furman* guidelines.

Five named defendants were each convicted of murder and sentenced to death in each of the five respective states: Georgia, North Carolina, Louisiana, Texas, and Florida. Those representing the five defendants in each of the five cases believed that the Court was willing to go further than it had in *Furman.*[53] Specifically the attorneys hoped that once and for all that the high court would rule that capital punishment was cruel and unusual punishment and that it violated the Eighth Amendment. However the Court responded that "The most marked indication of society's endorsement of the death penalty for murder is the legislative response to *Furman.*" Both Congress and 35 states had complied with the Court's dictates in *Furman* by either specifying factors to be weighed and procedures to be followed when imposing a death sentence, or dictating that the death penalty would be mandatory for specific crimes. Moreover, a California referendum had overturned the California Supreme Court's earlier decision in *California v. Anderson* which had ruled that the death penalty violated the California constitution, thus reinstating capital punishment in that very populous state. The fact that juries remained willing to impose the death penalty also contributed to the Court's conclusion that American society did not believe in 1976 that the death penalty was unconstitutional.

In the *Gregg* decision and its four companion cases the Court also found that the death penalty "comports with the basic concept of human dignity at the core of the [Eighth] Amendment". The high court reasoned that the death penalty serves two principal social purposes—retribution and deterrence. "In part, capital punishment is an expression of society's moral outrage at particularly offensive conduct". But this outrage must be expressed in an ordered fashion, for America is a society of laws. Retribution is consistent with human dignity, because society believes that "certain crimes are themselves so grievous an affront to humanity that the only adequate response may be the penalty of death". And although it is

---

[53] *Gregg v. Georgia, Proffitt v. Florida, Jurek v. Texas, Woodson v. North Carolina,* and *Roberts v. Louisiana,* 428 U.S. 153 (1976)

difficult to determine statistically how much crime the death penalty actually deters, the Court found that in 1976 there was "no convincing empirical evidence" supporting either the view that the death penalty is an effective deterrent to crime or that it was not so effective. However the Court reasoned that it could not completely discount the possibility that for certain "carefully contemplated murderers", "the possible penalty of death may well enter into the cold calculus that precedes the decision to act". Finally, the Court could not say that death was always disproportionate to the crime of deliberately taking human life. "It is an extreme sanction, suitable to the most extreme of crimes."[54]

## *Godfrey v. Georgia*

In the late 1960s, the Supreme Court began "fine tuning" the way the death penalty was administered. To this effect, the Court heard two cases in 1968 dealing with the discretion given to the prosecutor and the jury in capital cases. The first case was *U.S. v. Jackson*,[55] where the Supreme Court heard arguments regarding a provision of the federal kidnapping statute requiring that the death penalty be imposed only upon recommendation of a jury. The Court held that this practice was unconstitutional because it encouraged defendants to waive their right to a jury trial to ensure they would not receive a death sentence.

The other 1968 case was *Witherspoon v. Illinois*.[56] In this case, the Supreme Court held that a potential juror's mere reservations about the death penalty were insufficient grounds to prevent that person from serving on the jury in a death penalty case. Jurors could be disqualified only if prosecutors could show that the juror's attitude toward capital punishment would prevent him or her from making an impartial decision about the punishment.

In 1971, the Supreme Court again addressed the problems associated with the role of jurors and their discretion in capital cases. The

---

[54] *Gregg v. Georgia, Proffitt v. Florida, Jurek v. Texas, Woodson v. North Carolina,* and *Roberts v. Louisiana,* 428 U.S. 153 (1976)
[55] *U.S. v. Jackson,* 390 U.S. 570 (1968)
[56] *Witherspoon v. Illinois,* 391 U.S. 510 (1968)

Court decided *Crampton v. Ohio* and *McGautha v. California.*[57] The defendants argued it was a violation of their Fourteenth Amendment right to due process for jurors to have unrestricted discretion in deciding whether the defendants should live or die, and such discretion resulted in arbitrary and capricious sentencing. Crampton also argued that it was unconstitutional to have his guilt and sentence determined in one set of deliberations, as the jurors in his case were instructed that a first-degree murder conviction would result in a death sentence. The Court, however, rejected these claims, thereby approving of unfettered jury discretion and a single proceeding to determine guilt and sentence. The Court stated that guiding capital sentencing discretion was "beyond present human ability."

In September 1977, Robert Franklin Godfrey and his wife had a heated argument. After Godfrey becoming drunk, Godfrey threatened his wife. She left to stay with relatives. Soon after, she secured a warrant against Godfrey for aggravated assault and also filed for a divorce. Later in the same month, they argued again, at which time the wife told Godfrey that she had no interest in reconciliation. Godfrey went to the mobile home owned by his wife's mother armed with a shotgun. He shot both his wife and her mother and hit his own daughter. Godfrey then called the police, told them what he had done and asked them to come and pick him up. The State indicted Godfrey on two counts of murder, and one count of aggravated assault. He pled not guilty, arguing temporary insanity. The jury rejected that claim and found Godfrey guilty. At the sentencing phase, the same jury sentenced him to the death on both counts of murder. Georgia law held that a person may be convicted of murder and sentenced to the death penalty if it was beyond a reasonable doubt that the offense had been committed "outrageously or wantonly vile, horrible, or inhuman in that it involved torture, depravity of the mind, or an aggressive battery to the victim." Upon appeal the Georgia Supreme Court affirmed. Godfrey claimed that the Georgia law governing the death penalty "arbitrary and capricious" in violation of the Eighth Amendment?

Justice Potter Stewart delivered the opinion of the 6-3 plurality.

---

[57] *Crampton v. Ohio* and *McGautha v. California*, consolidated under 402 U.S. 183 (1971)

The court held that the Georgia law was unconstitutionally vague and failed to properly distinguish between those cases that would be eligible for the death penalty and those that were ineligible. Moreover, the Court found no evidence that Godfrey's crimes displayed the elements required in the law. Justice Thurgood Marshall concurred in an opinion in which he argued not only that the law was unconstitutional, but also that a death penalty sentencing requires much more restrictive sentencing guidelines than were apparent in the Georgia state law. He also argued that the death penalty itself was unconstitutional under the Eighth and Fourteenth Amendment. Justice William J. Brennan, Jr., joined in the concurrence.

Chief Justice Warren E. Burger wrote a dissenting opinion and argued that the plurality's decision leads to death penalty sentences being imposed on a case-by-case basis, which is even more arbitrary than the Georgia law. In another dissenting opinion, Justice Byron R. White argued that the Georgia law provided strict enough requirements to ensure that the imposition of the death penalty was not disproportionate to the crime. He also argued that the Supreme Court should not interfere with the decisions of the Georgia Supreme Court when they are "responsibly and consistently interpreting state law." Justice William H. Rehnquist joined in the dissent.[58]

## Walton v. Arizona

On March 2, 1986, Jeffrey Alan Walton, Robert Hoover, and Sharold Ramsey went to a bar in Tucson intending to rob someone at random and steal that individual's car. The three robbed Thomas Powell at gunpoint and forced him into his car that they drove into the desert. They later stopped the car, forced Powell to lie on the ground, and Walton shot him in the head. After the body was found, the coroner determined that the shot did not kill Powell, but rather that he died from dehydration, starvation, and pneumonia from being left in the desert.

The jury found Walton guilty of first-degree murder. When Walton was sentenced the prosecution argued that two aggravating factors were present: the murder was committed in "an especially heinous, cruel, or

---

[58] *Godfrey v. Georgia*, 446 U.S. 420 (1980),

depraved manner" and for the purposes of financial gain. For its part the defense pleaded that mitigating factors were present in the form of Walton's history of substance abuse, possible sexual abuse as a child, and the fact that he was only 20 years old at the time of the trial. The court found that the aggravating factors were present, and the judge sentenced Walton to death.

The jury did not buy the defense arguments and sentenced Walton to death. Under Arizona state law a person who has been convicted of first-degree murder is given a separate sentencing hearing to determine whether the punishment will be death or life imprisonment. The court must determine whether aggravating or mitigating factors were present. The presiding judge may imposes the death sentence if he is convinced that one or more aggravating factors are proven to exist. The judge imposed the death penalty. The Arizona Supreme Court affirmed the conviction and penalty. Upon appeal the U. S. Supreme Court was asked to decide if the Arizona state statutes governing death penalty sentencing were constitutionally permitted under the Sixth Amendment?

Justice Byron R. White delivered the opinion of the 5-4 plurality. The high court held that the Arizona method of death penalty sentencing is not arbitrary and does not place an undue burden on the defendant. The burden the law placed on the defendant to prove mitigating circumstances exist is not unconstitutional because it does not lessen the burden on the prosecution to prove that aggravating circumstances exist. The Court also held that a determination by a judge rather than a jury is constitutional because a judge has a great deal more legal expertise than even a well-instructed jury and is better able to make fair determinations. The wording of the statute itself is sufficiently clear to prevent arbitrary sentencing.

In a concurring opinion, Justice Antonin Scalia argued that the judicial history of death penalty cases is based on contradictory lines of logic. The courts have attempted to reduce discretionary decision-making while at the same time affording each case individualized examination. Because the discretionary rule has less basis in judicial history, he argues that it should not be a consideration in the constitutionality of death penalty cases.

Justice William J. Brennan, Jr. wrote a dissenting opinion where he argued that the death penalty is always a cruel and unusual punishment. Justice Thurgood Marshall joined in the dissent. In his separate dissent, Justice Harry A. Blackmun wrote that the Arizona statute places an unconstitutional burden on the defendant to prove that the mitigating factors are "sufficiently substantial to call for leniency." A defendant can produce evidence of mitigating factors that will have no weight if a judge determines them to lack the necessary significance. He also argued that the wording of the Arizona statute was too vague to provide sufficient guidance to the sentencing judge. Justice Brennan, Justice Marshall, and Justice John Paul Stevens joined in the dissent. Justice Stevens wrote a separate dissent where he argued that the Sixth Amendment requires death penalty sentencing to be conducted by a jury rather than a judge. He also argued that the individual facts of a case should have a bearing on sentencing decisions and that to ignore the role of discretion in such decisions would be unjust.[59]

## *Harris v. Alabama*

Louise Harris was married to the victim, a deputy sheriff, and was also having an affair with Lorenzo McCarty. Harris asked McCarter to find someone to kill her husband, and McCarter to that end approached a co-worker, who refused and reported the solicitation to his supervisor. McCarter then found willing accomplices in Michael Sockwell and Alex Hood, who were paid $100 and given a vague promise of more money upon performance. On the appointed night, as her husband left for work on the night shift, Harris called McCarter on his beeper to alert him. McCarter and Hood sat in a car parked on a nearby street, and Sockwell hid in the bushes next to a stop sign. As the victim stopped his car at the intersection, Sockwell sprang forth and shot him, point blank, with a shotgun. Harris was arrested after questioning, and McCarter agreed to bear witness to the conspiracy in exchange for the prosecutor's promise not to seek the death penalty. McCarter testified that Harris had asked him to kill her husband so they could share in his death benefits, which totaled about $250,000. Alabama law permits the trial judge to impose capital punishment, but requires the judge to "consider" among other factors the

---

[59] *Walton V Arizona, 497 U.S. 639 (1990)*

advisory opinion of the trial jury. After convicting petitioner Harris of capital murder, the jury recommended that she be imprisoned for life without parole, but the trial judge sentenced her to death because he concluded that the circumstances of the crime outweighed all of the mitigating circumstances. Upon appeal the Alabama Court of Criminal Appeals affirmed the conviction and sentence, and rejected Harris' argument that the capital sentencing statute is unconstitutional. Harris had argued that because the statute does not specify what weight the judge must give to the jury's recommendation the statute therefore permits the arbitrary imposition of the death penalty. Upon further appeal the Alabama Supreme Court affirmed both the conviction and the sentence.[60]

Justice O'Connor delivered the verdict of the court. The U. S. Supreme Court upheld the sentence because it said that the Eighth Amendment does not require the State to define the weight the sentencing judge must give to an advisory jury verdict. The U.S. Supreme Court had already ruled that the trial judge, acting alone, may impose a capital sentence.[61] Therefore the Constitution is not violated when a State further requires the judge to consider a jury recommendation and trusts the judge to give it the proper weight. Alabama's capital sentencing scheme is much like Florida's, except that a Florida sentencing judge is required to give the jury's recommendations "great weight."[62] The Supreme Court has written favorably of the *Tedder* standard. The high court made clear that the hallmark of the analysis is not the particular weight a State chooses to place upon the jury's advice, but whether the scheme adequately channels the sentencer's discretion so as to prevent arbitrary results. Thus to impose the *Tedder* standard here would offend established principles governing the criteria to be considered by the sentencer.[63]

Thus the Supreme Court found Harris' arguments for requiring that "great weight" be given to the jury's advice are unpersuasive. First, Alabama cases reversing death sentences for prejudicial errors committed before the advisory jury do not demonstrate that the jury's role is in fact

---

[60] *Harris v State*, 632 So. 2d 503 (1992)
[61] *Spaziano v. Florida*, 468 U.S. 447 (1984)
[62] *Tedder v. State*, 322 So.2d 908 (1975)
[63] *Franklin v. Lynaugh*, 487 U.S. 164 (1988)

determinative, but simply that a sentence imposed by the judge is invalid if the recommendation on which it partially rests was rendered erroneously. Second, although statistics demonstrate that there have been only five cases in which an Alabama judge rejected an advisory verdict of death, compared to forty-seven instances where the judge imposed a death sentence over a jury recommendation of life, these numbers do not tell the whole story because they do not indicate, for example, how many cases in which a jury recommendation of life was adopted would have ended differently had the judge not been required to consider the jury's advice. Moreover, the statistics say little about whether the Alabama method is constitutional, a question which turns not solely on numerical tabulations of sentences, but rather on whether the penalties imposed are the product of properly guided discretion and not of arbitrary whim. Finally, apparent disparities in the weight given to jury verdicts in specific Alabama cases do not indicate that the judges have divergent understandings of the statutory requirement that such verdicts be considered; they simply reflect the fact that, in the subjective weighing process, the emphasis given to each decisional criterion must of necessity vary to account for the particular circumstances in each case. In any event, Harris does not show how these disparities affect her case.[64]

Justice Stevens filed a dissenting opinion. He wrote, "Alabama's capital sentencing statute is unique. In Alabama, unlike any other State in the Union, the trial judge has unbridled discretion to sentence the defendant to death even though a jury has determined that death is an inappropriate penalty, and even though no basis exists for believing that any other reasonable, properly instructed jury would impose a death sentence. Even if I accepted the reasoning of *Spaziano v. Florida* . . . which I do not . . . I would conclude that the complete absence of standards to guide the judge's consideration of the jury's verdict renders the statute invalid under the Eighth Amendment and the Due Process Clause of the Fourteenth Amendment."[65]

---

[64] *Harris v Alabama,* 513 U.S. 504 (1995)
[65] *Harris v Alabama,* 513 U.S. 504 (1995) at 515-16

# Limiting the Application
# of the Death Penalty

As we have seen, the history of various nations shows the imposition of capital punishment for a veritable plethora of infractions, some seemingly trivial to the reader in the twentieth century and beyond. The Jews of the Old Testament knew some thirty-six transgressions that the Lord God ordered to be punished by the imposition of death. There were well over a hundred crimes that could bring capital punishment into play in eighteenth century England.

Certain exclusions have long been established in the common law tradition of the English speaking nations. One class always excluded has been those judged mentally incompetent. That category includes mentally incompetents and those clinically insane. Writing for the U.S. Supreme Court in 1986 Justice Thurgood Marshall reaffirmed that exclusion for insanity. Questions of the eligibility of any one person for inclusion in a list of mentally incompetents is best left to mental health professionals not the courts.[66]

Nearly all ethical models that humankind has known have some concept of proportionality. When allowed at all it must be only for some major transgression, usually willful murder. The United States was slow in implementing nationwide restrictions on the imposition of the death

---

[66] *Ford v Wainwright*, 477 U. S. 399 (1986). In this case having been judged sane during his trial, he exhibited traits of insanity and was placed in a facility for the insane, Ford was later held to be sane, and thus liable for execution, by a circuit judge. Ford died during his last appeal.

penalty. Those limitations came in 1977.

## *Woodson v. North Carolina*

Petitioners were convicted of first-degree murder as the result of their participation in an armed robbery of a convenience food store where the cashier was killed and a customer was seriously wounded. The Supreme Court of North Carolina upheld their sentences under the new North Carolina statute, which required death sentences for all defendants convicted of that crime. Upon appeal to the U.S. Supreme Court *Certiorari* was granted challenging the constitutionality of the statute. The high court was asked to decide whether the North Carolina's statute imposing mandatory death sentence for a first-degree murder violate the Eighth and Fourteenth Amendments.

The Court concluded that mandatory death penalties are incompatible with contemporary values and cannot be applied in consistency with requirement that the State's power to punish "be exercised within the limits of civilized standards." Writing for the court, Justice Stewart penned "The belief no longer prevails that every offense in a like legal category calls for an identical punishment without regard to the past life and habits of a particular offender,"[67]

The court found another deficiency of North Carolina's mandatory death sentence statute: it failed to respond to *Furman v. Georgia*. Justice Stewart wrote, "The North Carolina statute fails to provide a constitutionally tolerable response to Furman's rejection of unbridled jury discretion in the imposition of capital sentences. Central to the limited holding in that case was the conviction that vesting a jury with standard-less sentencing power violated the Eighth and Fourteenth Amendments, yet that constitutional deficiency is not eliminated by the mere formal removal of all sentencing power from juries in capital cases. In view of the historic record, it may reasonably be assumed that many juries under mandatory statutes will continue to consider the grave consequences of a conviction in reaching verdict. But the North Carolina statute provides no standards to guide the jury in determining which murderers

---

[67] Citing *Williams v. New York*, 337 U. S. 241, 337 U. S. 247.

shall live and which shall die."[68]

The court also held that the Eight Amendment requires consideration of various aspects of the character of the individual offender and the circumstances of the particular offense as a "constitutionally indispensable part of the process of imposing the ultimate punishment of death". The North Carolina statute did not allow such a particularized approach.

Thus, the U.S. Supreme Court found that the North Carolina mandatory death penalty statute is in violation of the Eighth and Fourteenth Amendments and must be set aside.[69] Justice Stewart wrote the opinion of the court joined by Justices Powell, Stevens and Brennan. Justice Marshall again announced his total opposition to the death sentence. Justice White dissented joined by Justices Rehnquist and Burger.

## *Coker v. Georgia*

The U.S. Supreme Court limited the application of the death penalty in *Coker v. Georgia*[70] The petitioner Ehrlich Anthony Coker was already in prison for various felonies, including murder, rape, kidnapping, and aggravated assault. Coker escaped from the Ware Correctional Institution near Waycross, Georgia, on September 2, 1974. At approximately 11 o'clock that night, petitioner entered the house of Allen and Elnita Carver through an unlocked kitchen door. Threatening the couple with a "board," he tied up Mr. Carver in the bathroom, obtained a knife from the kitchen, and took Mr. Carver's money and the keys to the family car. Brandishing the knife and saying "you know what's going to happen to you if you try anything, don't you," Coker then raped Mrs. Carver. Soon thereafter, petitioner drove away in the Carver car, taking Mrs. Carver with him, which constituted kidnapping. Mr. Carver, freeing himself, notified the police; and not long thereafter petitioner was apprehended. Mrs. Carver was unharmed. The district attorney charged Coker with various crimes including the rape. Having been found competent to stand trial, he was tried. The jury returned a verdict of guilty,

[68] *Woodson v. North Carolina*, 428 U.S. 280 at 302-03 (1976)
[69] Woodson v. North Carolina, 428 U.S. 280 (1976)
[70] Coker v. Georgia, 433 U.S. 584 (1977)

rejecting his general plea of insanity. A sentencing hearing was then conducted specifically he was convicted of rape and other violent offenses and was sentenced to death on the rape charge. The sentencing jury also found that two aggravating factors were present: prior record, and rape committed during course of other crimes.

The Georgia Supreme Court affirmed petitioner's conviction and sentence.

The U.S. Supreme Court granted *certiorari* only on the one issue of whether the death penalty for the crime of rape violates the Eighth Amendment. The U.S. Supreme Court reversed. The Court held that the death penalty for the crime of rape is grossly disproportionate and therefore violates the Eighth Amendment as cruel and unusual punishment. A punishment is unconstitutionally excessive if it imposes nothing more than unnecessary pain and suffering, and is grossly out of proportion based on the severity of the crime. With regard to current standards on the issue, most states do not allow for the death penalty for rape, and Georgia juries have only imposed the death penalty for rape in a small number of cases. The death penalty for rape is grossly disproportionate because rape does not involve the taking of a life. The aggravating factors found by the sentencing jury do not change that analysis. Indeed, under Georgia law, a person who intentionally kills may not get the death penalty. Thus, it is illogical to allow such a punishment for rape, when no life was taken. In any event, the death penalty is under any circumstance cruel and unusual in violation of the Eighth and Fourteenth Amendments.

Justice Powell issued a concurring opinion. Ordinarily, death is disproportionate punishment for the crime of rape. Here, the crime was not committed with excessive brutality or lasting injury, therefore the plurality's conclusion was justified. However, the plurality went too far in finding that death is always disproportionate for the crime of rape.

Chief Justice Burger submitted a dissenting opinion. He charged that the Court was confusing its proper role in this case. The Court's job is not to effectuate the Justices' personal views on capital punishment, but to disseminate what the Constitution requires. Here, the Court substituted its own policy judgment for the legislative will of the Georgia legislature. Rape is not a minor crime. Thus, Georgia was constitutionally justified in determining that the death penalty is a proper punishment for that crime. Burger dissented because he believed that the proportionality principle the Court had engrafted onto the Eighth Amendment encroached too much on the legislative power of the states. Burger preferred to concentrate on the narrow facts of the case: was it proper for Georgia to impose the death penalty on Coker, a man who had escaped from prison while serving a sentence for murder and raped another young woman? "Whatever one's view may be as to the State's constitutional power to impose the death penalty upon a rapist who stands before the court convicted for the first time, this case reveals a chronic rapist whose continuing danger to the community is abundantly clear." He was joined in his dissent by Justice Rehnquist.

## *Lockett v. Ohio*

The Ohio death penalty statute provided that once a defendant is found guilty of aggravated murder with at least one of seven specified aggravating circumstances, the death penalty must be imposed unless, considering "the nature and circumstances of the offense and the history, character, and condition of the offender," the sentencing judge determines that at least one of the following circumstances is established by a preponderance of the evidence: (1) the victim induced or facilitated the offense; (2) it is unlikely that the offense would have been committed but for the fact that the offender was under duress, coercion, or strong provocation; or (3) the offense was primarily the product of the offender's psychosis or mental deficiency. Petitioner Lockett was convicted of aggravated murder with specifications that it was committed to escape apprehension for, and while committing or attempting to commit, aggravated robbery. Her death sentence was affirmed by the Ohio Supreme Court. Lockett appealed claiming that the statute did not give the sentencing judge a full opportunity to consider mitigating circumstances in capital cases as required by the Eighth and Fourteenth Amendments.

The opinion of the court was written by Chief Justice Burger. The U.S. Supreme Court held that the limited range of mitigating circumstances that may be considered under the Ohio death penalty statute is incompatible with the Eighth and Fourteenth Amendments. The Eighth and Fourteenth Amendments require that in all but the rarest kind of capital case, there not be precluded from considering as a mitigating factor, any aspect of a defendant's character or record and any of the circumstances of the offense that the defendant proffers as a basis for a sentence less than death.[71]

The need for treating each defendant in a capital case with the degree of respect due the uniqueness of the individual is far more important than in non-capital cases, particularly in view of the unavailability with respect to an executed capital sentence of such post-conviction mechanisms in non-capital cases as probation, parole, and work furloughs.[72]

The Ohio statute prevented evidence in capital cases from being given mitigating weight to aspects of the defendant's character and record and to the circumstances of the offense is illegal under the Eighth and Fourteenth Amendments.[73]

Moreover, the Ohio death penalty statute did not permit the type of individualized consideration of mitigating factors required by the Eighth and Fourteenth Amendments. Only the three factors specified in the statute can be considered in mitigation of the defendant's sentence, and, once it is determined that none of those factors is present, the statute mandates the death sentence.[74]

## Beck v. Alabama

Gilbert Beck was arrested and tried for murder during the course of a robbery in 1977. At trial, he admitted to robbery, but denied murder. Testimony reflected that he did not kill the victim.

But under Alabama's unique death penalty statute, juries were given only two choices: vote to convict and trigger an automatic death sentence, or vote to acquit and let the defendant go free. Beck was convicted of capital murder and sentenced to die.

---

[71] *Lockett v. Ohio,* 438 U.S. 586 at 604-05 (1978)
[72] Id. at 605
[73] Id at 605
[74] Id. at 606-08

The Southern Poverty Law Center appealed Beck's conviction, but the Alabama courts upheld the conviction and the statute. The United States Supreme Court issued *Certiorari.*

The Supreme Court said that failure to allow the jury to find Beck guilty of something less serious than capital murder, such as manslaughter or first-degree murder, created the risk that the jury would convict simply to avoid letting the defendant go free. It held that the death sentence may not constitutionally be imposed after a jury verdict of guilt of a capital offense where the jury was not permitted to consider a verdict of guilt of a lesser included offense.[75]

Justice Stevens wrote the opinion of the court, saying that providing the jury with the "third option" of convicting on a lesser included offense ensures that the jury will accord the defendant the full benefit of the reasonable doubt standard. This procedural safeguard is especially important in cases such as this one. For when the evidence establishes that the defendant is guilty of a serious, violent offense but leaves some doubt as to an element justifying conviction of a capital offense, the failure to give the jury such a "third option" inevitably enhances the risk of an unwarranted conviction. Such a risk cannot be tolerated in a case in which the defendant's life is at stake.[76]

Both the judge's instructions and the apparently mandatory nature of the death penalty both interjected irrelevant considerations into the fact-finding process, diverting the jury's attention from the central issue of whether the State has satisfied its burden of proving beyond a reasonable doubt that the defendant is guilty of a capital crime.

The unavailability of the "third option" may encourage the jury to convict for an impermissible reason -- its belief that the defendant is guilty of some serious crime and should be punished. Or the apparently mandatory nature of the death penalty may encourage the jury to acquit because, whatever his crime, the defendant does not deserve death.[77]

---

[75] *Beck v Alabama,* 447 U. S. 625 at 646 (1980).
[76] Id at 638.
[77] Id at 643

# *Enmund v. Florida*

Sampson and Jeanette Armstrong rang the doorbell of Thomas and Eunice Kersey, who lived at a farmhouse in Central Florida. When Thomas Kersey answered, Sampson Armstrong held him at gunpoint while Jeanette took his money. Eunice came out with a gun and shot Jeanette, wounding her. Sampson shot back and killed both of the Kerseys. Meanwhile Earl Enmund sat outside in the getaway car. The Armstrongs took all the Kerseys' money and then went back to the getaway car Enmund was driving. Enmund and the Armstrongs were all indicted for first-degree murder and robbery. The judge instructed the jury that under Florida law, killing a human being while engaged in the perpetration or in the attempt to perpetrate a robbery is first-degree murder. Jeanette and Sampson Armstrong were convicted of first-degree murder.

At a separate penalty hearing, the trial judge found that the murders were committed for pecuniary gain and were especially heinous, atrocious, or cruel. No statutory mitigating factors applied, so the judge sentenced Enmund to death. On appeal, the Florida Supreme Court rejected Enmund's contention that his death sentence was inappropriate because he did not kill or intend to kill the Kerseys. It held that the "felony murder rule and the law of principals combine to make a felon generally responsible for the lethal acts of his co-felon."

Certiorari granted, the U. S. Supreme Court heard the Enmund appeal. Justice White delivered the opinion of the Court. The question before the Court was whether death is a valid penalty under the Eighth and Fourteenth Amendments for one who neither took life, attempted to take life, nor intended to take life. The majority of the court found that the record did not support a finding that Enmund killed or attempted to kill the Kerseys, and the record did not support a finding that Enmund intended to participate in the killing or facilitate the killing. Accordingly, the Court held the imposition of a sentence of death upon Enmund was prohibited by the Eighth Amendment because Enmund only "aided and abetted a felony in the course of which a murder is committed by others but who does not himself kill, attempt to kill, or intend that a killing take place or that lethal force will be employed."

Justice Brennan delivered a concurring opinion, holding that the death penalty in and of itself is a cruel and unusual punishment and thus is prohibited by the Eighth Amendment in all circumstances. Justice O'Connor, joined by Chief Justice Burger, Justice Powell, and Justice Rehnquist, delivered the dissenting opinion, holding that the majority opinion interfered with state criteria for assessing guilt.[78]

## *Spaziano v Florida*

Having refused Certiorari in 1981, the U. S. Supreme Court granted it in the second case, and the Court heard Spaziano's appeal of his death sentence. Florida had tried Spaziano for first-degree murder. It might have tried him on lesser charges but the statute of limitations had expired. Florida offered to offer these alternatives to the jury provided would waive the statute of limitations which he refused to do. The trial proceeded with the jury having only the simple choice of finding him guilty on the single charge or acquitting him. The jury convicted Spaziano and recommended a sentence of life imprisonment. Florida law makes the jury's recommendation merely that, a recommendation, and requires the judge to examine the aggravating and mitigating factors and thus gives the judge the power to override the jury and impose the death penalty. The judge exercised the right to override the jury and imposed a death sentence.[79]

The high court held that it was not error for the trial judge to refuse to instruct the jury on lesser included offenses. While Beck v. Alabama had recognized the risk of an unwarranted conviction that is created when the jury is deprived of the "third option" of convicting the defendant of a lesser included offense that requirement did not apply in this case. Petitioner's general premise that a criminal defendant may not be required to waive a substantive right - here the right to a statute of limitations - as a condition for receiving an otherwise constitutionally fair trial did not apply to petitioner's situation. Where no lesser offense exists, including the non-viable instruction detracts from, rather than enhances, the rationality of the process. The defendant has the option of waiving the expired statute of limitations on lesser included offenses in order to have

---

[78] Enmund v Florida, 458 U.S. 782
[79] *Spaziano v Florida*, 468 U.S. 447 (1984)

the jury instructed on those offenses, or of asserting the statute of limitations.[80]

The court also held that there is no constitutional requirement that a jury's recommendation of life imprisonment in a capital case be final so as to preclude the trial judge from overriding the jury's recommendation and imposing the death sentence. The fundamental issue in a capital sentencing proceeding is the determination of the appropriate punishment to be imposed on an individual, and the Sixth Amendment does not guarantee a right to a jury determination of that issue. Nothing in the safeguards against arbitrary and discriminatory application of the death penalty necessitated by the qualitative difference of the penalty requires that the sentence be imposed by a jury. And the purposes of the death penalty are not frustrated by, or inconsistent with, a scheme in which imposition of the penalty is determined by a judge. The fact that the majority of jurisdictions with capital sentencing statutes give the life-or-death decision to the jury does not establish that contemporary standards of fairness and decency are offended by the jury override. The Eighth Amendment is not violated every time a State reaches a conclusion different from a majority of its sisters over how best to administer its criminal laws.[81]

The determination that there is no constitutional imperative that a jury have the responsibility of deciding whether the death penalty should be imposed also disposes of petitioner's double jeopardy challenge to the jury-override procedure. If the judge is vested with sole responsibility for imposing the penalty, the judge's advice does not become a judgment simply because it comes from the jury. Application of the Florida standards allowing a trial court to cover-ride a jury's recommendation of a life sentence does not violate the constitutional requirement of reliability in capital sentencing.[82]

## *Sumner v. Shuman*

In 1958 Raymond Wallace Shuman was convicted in a Nevada

---

[80] Id at 454-457.
[81] Id at 457-465.
[82] Id at 465

state court of first-degree murder for the shooting death of a truck-driver during a roadside robbery. He was sentenced to life imprisonment without possibility of parole. At that time the trial jury had three sentencing options: the death penalty; of life imprisonment with the possibility of parole; or life sentence without the possibility of parole. While serving his life sentence, Shuman was convicted of capital murder for the killing of a fellow inmate. Based on Nevada law then in effect, Shuman's conviction mandated that he be sentenced to death.

The Nevada Supreme Court affirmed Shuman's conviction and the imposition of the death penalty. It specifically rejected respondent's claims of error, including his objection that the mandatory imposition of the death sentence violated his rights under the Eighth and Fourteenth Amendments. Shuman unsuccessfully pursued his challenge to the mandatory capital-punishment statute in a state habeas petition.[83]

After exhausting state remedies, Shuman filed a petition in Federal District Court seeking habeas corpus relief. The District Court rejected all his claims except his challenge to the constitutionality of the mandatorily imposed death sentence. The District Court acknowledged that in several cases the Supreme Court had reserved judgment on the question whether a mandatory death penalty may be justified in the case of an inmate serving a life sentence who is convicted of murder. The District Court reasoned that sentencing authorities should have been permitted to consider any relevant mitigating circumstance in their decision. Thus, Shuman's death sentence was invalid. It found that the availability of a non-mandatory death penalty was a sufficient deterrent to life-term inmates. It wrote that making a death sentence mandatory "only serves to give the imposition of the death sentence the air of arbitrariness and caprice." It held that the law in effect at the time Shuman was sentenced to death therefore violated the Eighth and Fourteenth Amendments, and it ordered that Shuman's death sentence be vacated.[84]

Justice Blackmun delivered the opinion of the Court, joined by Justices Brennan, Marshall, Powell, Stevens, and O'Connor. It held that

---

[83] *Shuman v. State,* 94 Nev. 265, 578 P.2d 1183 (1978).
[84] *Shuman v. Wolff,* 571 F.Supp. 213 (Nev. 1983).

under the individualized capital-sentencing doctrine, it is constitutionally required that the sentencing authority consider, as a mitigating factor, any aspect of the defendant's character or record and any of the circumstances of the particular offense. A statute that mandates the death penalty for a prison inmate who is convicted of murder while serving a life sentence without possibility of parole violates the Eighth and Fourteenth Amendments.

Justice White dissented, joined by Chief Justice Rehnquist and Justice Scalia. Justice White wrote,

> Until today, the Court has never held that the Constitution prohibits a State from identifying an especially aggravated and exceedingly narrow category of first-degree murder, such as the crime for which respondent stands convicted, and determining as a matter of law and social policy that no combination of mitigating factors, short of an actual defense to the crime charged, could ever warrant reduction of a sentence of death. I thus do not accept the majority's assertion that "[t]he fact that a life-term inmate is convicted of murder does not reflect whether any circumstance existed at the time of the murder that may have lessened his responsibility for his acts even though it could not stand as a legal defense to the murder charge." . . . An inmate serving a life sentence who is convicted of capital murder and who is legally responsible for his actions, that is, one who does not have a meritorious defense recognized as relieving the inmate of such responsibility, has, in my view, no constitutional right to persuade the sentencer to impose essentially no punishment at all for taking the life of another, whether guard or inmate. . . . I also reject the majority's assertion that this kind of mandatory capital-sentencing scheme is not necessary as a deterrent because the inmate who commits capital murder is still subject to the death penalty for that crime.[85]

---

[85] *Sumner v Shuman*, 483 U.S. 66 (1987)

## *Tison v. Arizona*

Gary Tison had been sentenced to life imprisonment for the murder of a guard whom he killed in the course of a prison escape. After spending a number of years in jail, Tison's wife, their three sons, Tison's brother and other relatives engineered Gary's escape. His three sons, Donald, Ricky, and Raymond, plotted to break him and his cellmate, Randy Greenawalt, out of prison. On July 30, 1978, the sons entered the prison for a visit, taking advantage of a policy that allowed an informal picnic setting for weekend family visits, carrying an ice chest packed with revolvers and sawed-off shotguns. One of them aimed a sawed-off shotgun at a lobby guard. Greenawalt helped in the escape by cutting off telephones and alarm systems.

During the escape no shots were fired. During the escape, the getaway car had a flat tire. They flagged down a passing motorist and stole his car. In the car were John Lyons, his wife Donnelda, his two-year-old son Christopher and his 15-year-old niece, Theresa Tyson. Tison and his former cellmate Randy Greenawalt shot and killed all four passengers. The petitioners were Gary's sons. Despite not personally killing anyone, both were convicted of armed robbery, kidnapping, car theft and capital murder. Under Arizona law, a killing which occurs during the perpetration of robbery or kidnapping is capital murder and each participant in the kidnapping or robbery is legally responsible for the acts of his accomplices. Both the sons were sentenced to death for the four murders.[86]

When the sentences were upheld by the highest court in Arizona the men appealed to the federal courts. The issue before the U. S. Supreme Court was: Does the Eighth Amendment of the United States Constitution prohibit the death penalty where the defendant participated substantially in the crime, but whose mental state is one of reckless indifference to the value of human life, rather than a mental state reflecting an intent to kill?

Justice Sandra Day O'Connor wrote the Opinion of the Court in which Justices Rehnquist, White, Powell, and Scalia joined. The Court held that the death penalty may be imposed where there exists no specific

---

[86] "Death in the Desert". *Time*. September 4, 1978.

intent to kill but rather, the defendant knowingly and substantially participated in criminal activities known to carry a grave risk of death. The Petitioners aided in bringing an arsenal of lethal weapons to a prison in order to arm two convicted murderers for the purpose of escaping. One petitioner, Raymond Tison, flagged down the victims, robbed the victims, and guarded them at gunpoint. He then watched the killing without making an effort to assist the victims. The role of the other petitioner, Ricky Tison, was substantially the same. The Court wrote, "the reckless disregard for human life implicit in knowingly engaging in criminal activities known to carry a grave risk of death represents a highly culpable mental state, a mental state that may be taken into account in making a capital sentencing judgment when that conduct causes its natural, though also not inevitable, lethal result."

Justice William Brennan wrote a Dissenting Opinion, with which Justice Thurgood Marshall, Justice Harry Blackmun, and Justice John Paul Stevens joined. In his dissent Justice Brennan pointed out that intent should be irrelevant since the petitioners did not commit an act that killed anyone. He complained that the majority mistakenly focused on their mental state of acts committed by others.[87]

The state eventually reduced the death penalties of Ricky and Raymond Tison to life sentences because they were both under 20 at the time of the crimes. Greenawalt was executed in 1997.

## *Lowenfield v. Phelps*

Leslie Lowenfield, a native of Guyana, came to Louisiana from Canada in June 1981 and met the primary victim, Sheila Thomas, a deputy sheriff in Jefferson Parish, Louisiana, shortly thereafter. Ms. Thomas, along with her young daughter, victim Shantell Osborne, moved in with Lowenfield later in the summer of 1981. Lowenfield and Ms. Thomas lived together off and on for approximately one year. During this year, Ms. Thomas left Lowenfield on three separate occasions and returned to live with her mother. Lowenfield became increasingly bitter following each separation. When Ms. Thomas returned to her mother's home for the last

---

[87] *Tison v Arizona*, 481 U.S. 137, 107 S. Ct. 1676 (1987)

time, he repeatedly threatened and harassed Ms. Thomas and her mother, victim, Myrtle Griffin. In the late afternoon of August 30, 1982, Owen Griffin, Sheila Thomas' stepfather, was in a vacant lot near his home in Marrero, Louisiana playing cards with friends. Owen Griffin heard shots ring out from his home, and ran to the house and rushed inside whereupon more shots rang out. When the police arrived, they found five bodies sprawled about the living area of the house; they found the bodies of Sheila Thomas, her four-year old daughter Shantell, Owen Griffin, his wife Myrtle Griffin, and Carl Osborne, the father of Shantell. All of the victims had sustained multiple gunshot wounds; each had been shot in the head at close range.[88]

In 1986 having killed five people Lowenfield was convicted of manslaughter and first-degree murder. The jury had difficulty obtaining a verdict. The trial court gave the jury a supplemental charge and sent them back to deliberate. After the charge, the jury returned the convictions and thereafter, sentenced petitioner to death. After availing all of his state remedies, petitioner sought habeas corpus relief in federal court claiming that the jury was improperly coerced by the supplemental charge given by the state court. The lower courts denied the request for habeas corpus.[89]

Justice Rehnquist wrote the Opinion of the Court and was joined by Justices White, Blackmun, O'Connor, and Scalia; and in part by Justice Stevens. It held that the death sentence does not violate the Eighth Amendment simply because the single statutory "aggravating circumstance" found by the jury duplicates an element of the underlying offense of first-degree murder. To pass constitutional muster, a capital sentencing scheme must "genuinely narrow the class of persons eligible for the death penalty, and must reasonably justify the imposition of a more severe sentence on the defendant compared to others found guilty of murder."[90]

The Court held that the trial judge's polling of the jury and

[88] "Louisiana Executes Man, 34, Convicted of Murdering Five". *New York Times.* 13 April 1988.
[89] *State v. Lowenfield*, 495 So.2d 1245 (La.1985); 817 F.2d 285 (1987)
[90] *Lowenfield v. Phelps*, 484 U.S. 231 (1988)

supplemental Allen instruction did not coerce the jury to return a verdict of guilty. The Court also rejected a challenge that Louisiana's death penalty statute did not sufficiently narrow the category of defendants who are eligible for the death penalty. The aggravating circumstance in the case, intentionally killing more than one person was found by the jury in the guilt phase after returning 3 first degree murder verdicts. The Court held that the two jury polls and the supplemental charge did not impermissibly coerce the jury to return a death sentence, and that the death sentence does not violate the Eighth Amendment simply because the single statutory "aggravating circumstance" found by the jury duplicates an element of the underlying offense of first-degree murder.

The dissenting opinion was filed by Justice Thurgood Marshall and joined by Justice Brennan and in part by Justice Stevens. Justice Marshall wrote,

> Adhering to my view that the death penalty is in all circumstances cruel and unusual punishment prohibited by the Eighth and Fourteenth Amendments, . . . I would vacate the decision below insofar as it left undisturbed the death sentence imposed in this case. Even if I did not hold this view, I would vacate petitioner's sentence of death for two independent reasons. First, the jury that sentenced Leslie Lowenfield was subjected during the penalty phase of the trial to a combination of practices that courts have viewed as coercive in far less sensitive situations. The use of these practices in this case presents an unacceptable risk that the jury returned a sentence of death for reasons having nothing to do with proper constitutional considerations. Second, even in the absence of coercion, the jury's sentence of death could not stand because it was based on a single statutory aggravating circumstance that duplicated an element of petitioner's underlying offense. This duplication prevented Louisiana's sentencing scheme from adequately guiding the discretion of the sentencing jury in this case and relieved the jury of the requisite sense of responsibility for its sentencing decision. As we have recognized frequently in the past, such failings may have the effect of impermissibly biasing the sentencing process in favor of death in violation of the

Eighth and the Fourteenth Amendments.

## *Kennedy v. Louisiana*

In 2008 in *Kennedy v. Louisiana*[91], the court expanded *Coker,* ruling that the death penalty is unconstitutional in all cases that do not involve murder or crimes against the State. Patrick O'Neal Kennedy from Harvey, Louisiana in Greater New Orleans, was sentenced to death after being convicted of raping and sodomizing his eight-year-old stepdaughter. The rape, taking place in March 1998, was uncommonly brutal: it tore the victim's perineum "from her vaginal opening to her anal opening. [It] tore her vagina on the interior such that it separated partially from her cervix and allowed her rectum to protrude into her vagina. Invasive emergency surgery was required to repair these injuries." Kennedy maintained that the battery was committed by two neighborhood boys, and refused to plead guilty when a deal was offered to spare him from a death sentence. Nevertheless, he was convicted in 2003 and sentenced under a 1995 Louisiana law that allowed the death penalty for the rape of a child under the age of 12.

On appeal, Kennedy challenged the constitutionality of executing a person solely for child rape, and the Louisiana Supreme Court rejected the challenge on the grounds that the death penalty was not too harsh for such a heinous offense. The Louisiana Supreme Court held that it is constitutional to impose the death penalty for rape if the victim is a child. Ruling on an appeal brought in the case of defendant Patrick Kennedy, Justice Jeffrey Victory wrote for the court that the Louisiana law allowing the imposition of the death penalty under those circumstances was consistent with Coker because an aggravating circumstance, the age of the victim, justified the death penalty.

Jeffrey L. Fisher, a Stanford Law School professor appealed the Louisiana decision to the U.S. Supreme Court. He played the race card effectively, arguing that state courts singled out black child rapists for imposition of the death sentence significantly more frequently that they did for than white rapists. The Supreme Court issued

---

[91] *Kennedy v. Louisiana,* 554 U.S. 407 (2008)

Certiorari on January 4, 2008.

Ass the case developed counsels pitted the Eighth Amendment definition of "cruel and unusual punishment" against states' rights as defined in the Tenth Amendment. The central issue was whether states may constitutionally impose the death penalty for any crime other than murder as a principle of a state's right to impose punishment as they chose. Jefferson Parish, Louisiana, assistant district attorney Juliet L. Clark argued for the State of Louisiana and Texas Solicitor General Ted Cruz argued for the State of Texas and other *amicus curiae* states.

The Supreme Court issued its decision on 25 June 2008. The heavily and ideologically divided court split 5–4. The bare majority decision, authored by Justice Kennedy, held that "[t]he Eighth Amendment bars Louisiana from imposing the death penalty for the rape of a child where the crime did not result, and was not intended to result, in the victim's death." Kennedy explained that the imposition of the death penalty had to rest on national consensus, and that as only six States permitted the death penalty for child rape. Thus, no such consensus existed. "Unlike Louisiana, those states all require that a defendant have a previous rape conviction or some other aggravating factor in order to be subject to the death penalty, and no one has yet been sentenced to death under any of the laws." The opinion, which was joined by the court's four more liberal judges, went on to state, "The court concludes that there is a distinction between intentional first–degree murder, on the one hand, and non–homicide crimes against individuals, even including child rape, on the other. The latter crimes may be devastating in their harm, as here, but in terms of moral depravity and of the injury to the person and to the public, they cannot compare to murder in their severity and irrevocability." The opinion concluded that in cases of crimes against individuals, "the death penalty should not be expanded to instances where the victim's life was not taken." However, Kennedy wrote, "We do not address, for example, crimes defining and punishing treason, espionage, terrorism, and drug kingpin activity, which are offenses against the State."

Justices Brennan and Marshall concurred in the judgment because the case struck down a death penalty. The was in agreement with their view that the death penalty is in and of itself cruel and unusual punishment.

Justice Powell concurred in the judgment, but he emphasized that the death penalty may be appropriate for rape if there are aggravating circumstances.

The dissenting opinion was the handiwork of Justice Alito. He sharply criticized the majority for usurping the role of the legislature. Alito argued that Kennedy's rationale for defining national consensus was flawed, because the previous *Coker* decision had "stunted legislative consideration of the question whether the death penalty for the targeted offense of raping a young child is consistent with prevailing standards of decency." Alito followed the reasoning of former Chief Justice Warren Burger, who had dissented from *Coker* because it, in his view, prevented a full debate over the uses of the recently reinstated death penalty. In this vein, Alito also argued that "The Eighth Amendment protects the right of an accused. It does not authorize this Court to strike down federal or state criminal laws on the ground that they are not in the best interests of crime victims or the broader society."

In two recent cases, the Supreme Court has limited who may be executed. In 2002 in *Atkins v. Virginia*, the Supreme Court decided that executing people with intellectual disabilities is cruel and unusual punishment, and thus violates the Eighth Amendment. Before this decision, between 1984 and 1992, forty-four people with intellectual disabilities were executed in the United States.

Daryl Renard Atkins, was convicted of abduction, armed robbery, and capital murder, and sentenced to death. At approximately midnight on August 16, 1996, Atkins and William Jones, armed with a semiautomatic handgun, abducted Eric Nesbitt, robbed him of the money he possessed, drove him to an automated teller machine in his pickup truck where cameras recorded their withdrawal of additional cash, and then took him to an isolated location where they was shot Nesbitt eight times, killing him.

Jones and Atkins both testified in the guilt phase of the first Atkins trial. Each confirmed the essential details in the other's account of the incident, with the important exception that each stated that the other had actually shot and killed Nesbitt. Jones' testimony was both more coherent and credible than that of Atkins. At the penalty phase of the trial, the State introduced victim impact evidence and proved two aggravating circumstances: "future dangerousness" and "vileness of the offense." To prove future dangerousness, the State relied on Atkins' prior felony convictions as well as the testimony of.

In issuing a Writ of Certiorari the Supreme Court of the United States thought that there was a serious question as to whether there was justification for the death penalty applies to mentally retarded offenders. The high court inquired as to "the social purposes served by the death penalty. Unless the imposition of the death penalty on a mentally retarded person "measurably contributes" to some clearly defined goal, it 'is nothing more than the purposeless and needless imposition of pain and suffering,' and hence an unconstitutional punishment."[92]

With respect to retribution the severity of the appropriate punishment necessarily depends on the culpability of the offender. Since Gregg, our jurisprudence has consistently confined the imposition of the death penalty to a narrow category of the most serious crimes. If the culpability of the average murderer is insufficient to justify the most extreme sanction available to the State, the lesser culpability of the mentally retarded offender surely does not merit that form of retribution. Thus, pursuant to the narrowing tendencies of American jurisprudence, the court sought to ensure that only the most deserving of execution are put to death, an exclusion for the mentally retarded is appropriate.

Again citing Enmund, with respect to deterrence, the court wrote, "it seems likely that 'capital punishment can serve as a deterrent only when murder is the result of premeditation and deliberation,'" Exempting the mentally retarded from that punishment will not affect the "cold calculus that precedes the decision" of other potential murderers. Indeed, that sort of calculus is at the opposite end of the spectrum from behavior of mentally retarded offenders. The theory of deterrence in capital sentencing is predicated upon the notion that the increased severity of the punishment will inhibit criminal actors from carrying out murderous conduct. Yet it is the same cognitive and behavioral impairments that make these defendants less morally culpable--for example, the diminished ability to understand and process information, to learn from experience, to engage in logical

---

[92] Citing *Enmund v Florida,* 458 U. S. 782, (1982). The court in this case relied heavily on *Enmund.*

reasoning, or to control impulses--that also make it less likely that they can process the information of the possibility of execution as a penalty and, as a result, control their conduct based upon that information. Nor will exempting the mentally retarded from execution lessen the deterrent effect of the death penalty with respect to offenders who are not mentally retarded. Such individuals are unprotected by the exemption and will continue to face the threat of execution. Thus, executing the mentally retarded will not measurably further the goal of deterrence.[93]

The reduced capacity of mentally retarded offenders provided yet another justification for a rule making such offenders ineligible for the death penalty. The risk "that the death penalty will be imposed in spite of factors which may call for a less severe penalty,"[94] is enhanced by the possibility of false confessions. The diminished ability of mentally retarded defendants to make a persuasive showing of mitigation in the face of prosecutorial evidence of one or more aggravating factors. Mentally retarded defendants may be less able to give meaningful assistance to their counsel and are typically poor witnesses, and their demeanor may create an unwarranted impression of lack of remorse for their crimes.

The high court expressed admiration for the judgment of those "legislatures that have recently addressed the matter" and concluded that death is not a suitable punishment for a mentally retarded criminal. We are not persuaded that the execution of mentally retarded criminals will measurably advance the deterrent or the retributive purpose of the death penalty." The court therefore concluded that such punishment is excessive and that the Constitution "places a substantive restriction on the State's power to take the life" of a mentally retarded offender and the judgment of the Virginia Supreme Court was reversed.[95]

Chief Justice Rehnquist prepared a dissenting opinion, with which Justice Scalia and Justice Thomas joined. Justice Rehnquist wrote, "There are strong reasons for limiting our inquiry into what constitutes an evolving standard of decency under the Eighth Amendment to the laws

---

[93] See also *Gregg v Georgia*, 428 U. S. 153 (1976)

[94] *Lockett v. Ohio*, 438 U. S. 586, (1978)

[95] *Atkins v Virginia*, 477 U. S., at 405 (2002)

passed by legislatures and the practices of sentencing juries in America. Here, the Court goes beyond these well-established objective indicators of contemporary values. It finds "further support to [its] conclusion" that a national consensus has developed against imposing the death penalty on all mentally retarded defendants in international opinion, the views of professional and religious organizations, and opinion polls not demonstrated to be reliable. . . . Believing this view to be seriously mistaken, I dissent."

The Atkins case reversed the history of executions of mentally retarded persons. Before Atkins, there was the shameful case of Jerome Bowden. This man was identified as having mental retardation when he was 14-years old. Bowden was scheduled for imminent execution in Georgia in June of 1986. The Georgia Board of Pardons and Paroles granted a stay following public protests which opposed his execution. A psychologist selected by the State evaluated Bowden and determined that he had an IQ of 65, which is consistent with severe mental retardation. Nevertheless, the board lifted the stay and Bowden was executed the following day. The board had concluded that Bowden understood the nature of his crime and his punishment, and therefore his execution, despite his mental deficiencies, was permissible.[96]

Then in 2005 in *Roper v. Simmons*, the Supreme Court held that it was unconstitutional to execute a person who was younger than 18 at the time the crime was committed. A 1988 Supreme Court decision, *Thompson v. Oklahoma*,[97] had barred execution of offenders under the age of 16. In 1989, another case, *Stanford v. Kentucky*,[98] had upheld the possibility of capital punishment for offenders who were 16 or 17 years old when they committed the capital offense.

When he was 17 year of age Simmons planned and committed a capital murder. Following his capture, arrest, and trial he had turned 18. Because of the nature of the crime the jury sentenced Simmons to death. His direct appeal and subsequent petitions for state and federal post-

---

[96] "Bowden's Execution Stirs Protest, "*Atlanta Journal*, 13, October1986
[97] *Thompson v. Oklahoma*, 487 U.S. 815 (1988).
[98] *Stanford v. Kentucky*, 492 U.S. 361 (1989).

conviction relief were rejected. Meanwhile the United States Supreme Court held that the Eighth Amendment, applicable to the States through the Fourteenth Amendment, prohibits the execution of a mentally retarded person.[99] Simmons filed a new petition for state post-conviction relief, arguing that Atkins' reasoning established that the Constitution prohibits the execution of a juvenile who was under 18 when he committed his crime. The Missouri Supreme Court agreed and set aside Simmons' death sentence replacing it with life imprisonment without eligibility for release. It rejected the assertion that the Constitution bars capital punishment for juvenile offenders younger than 18, but a national consensus has developed against the execution of those offenders since Stanford.[100]

The U.S. Supreme Court heard the case and held that the Eighth and Fourteenth Amendments forbid imposition of the death penalty on offenders who were under the age of 18 when their crimes were committed. The Court ruled that the death penalty constitutes an excessive sanction for juvenile offenders. Capital punishment must be limited to those offenders who commit "a narrow category of the most serious crimes" and whose extreme culpability makes them "the most deserving of execution." As in *Atkins*, the Supreme Court found that the objective indication of national consensus here suggested the rejection of the juvenile death penalty in the majority of States. The high court noted the infrequency of its use even where it remained on the books. It found that there was a consistent trend toward abolition of this practice.

Justice O'Connor filed a dissenting opinion in which she wrote, "The Court's decision today establishes a categorical rule forbidding the execution of any offender for any crime committed before his 18th birthday, no matter how deliberate, wanton, or cruel the offense. Neither the objective evidence of contemporary societal values, nor the Court's moral proportionality analysis, nor the two in tandem suffice to justify this ruling." Justice Scalia also filed a dissenting opinion, in which Chief Justice Rehnquist and Justice joined. The Scalia dissent followed familiar lines, holding

---

[99] *Atkins v. Virginia*, 536 U.S. 304
[100] *Stanford v. Kentucky*, 492 U.S. 361

that the justices were substituting their own beliefs for the will of legislatures.

# Age Criteria for
# Imposing Capital Punishment

Over the decades, and increasingly in more recent years, American court have held that there are three general differences between juveniles under 18 and adults. Court have held that juvenile offenders cannot with reliability be classified among the worst offenders.[101] First, as any parent knows and as the scientific and sociological studies respondent and his *amici* cite tend to confirm, a lack of maturity and an underdeveloped sense of responsibility are found in youth more often than in adults and are more understandable among the young. These qualities often result in impetuous and ill-considered actions and decisions. Even a normal 16-year-old customarily lacks the maturity of an adult. It has been noted that "adolescents are over represented statistically in virtually every category of reckless behavior." [102] In recognition of the comparative immaturity and irresponsibility of juveniles, almost every State prohibits those under 18 years of age from voting, serving on juries, or marrying without parental consent.

The second difference the courts have noticed is that juveniles are more vulnerable or susceptible to negative influences and outside pressures, including peer pressure. Research has shown that youth is a time and condition of life when a person may be most susceptible to influence and to psychological damage. Juveniles tend to have less control, or less

---

[101] *Roper v Simmons*, 543 U.S. 551 (2005)

[102] Arnett, Jeffrey, "Reckless Behavior in Adolescence: A Developmental Perspective," *Developmental Review,* 12: 339-73 (1992).

experience with control, over their own environment. Research has also shown that legal minors, lack the freedom that adults have to extricate themselves from a criminogenic setting.[103]

The third broad difference is that the character of a juvenile is not as well formed as that of an adult. The personality traits of juveniles are more transitory, less fixed.[104]

## Juvenile Executions

The first execution of a juvenile offender was in 1642 with Thomas Graunger in the Plymouth Colony. In the 350 plus years since that time, a total of approximately 365 persons have been executed for juvenile crimes, constituting 1.8% of roughly 20,000 confirmed American executions since 1608. Twenty-two of these executions for juvenile crimes have been imposed since the reinstatement of the death penalty in 1976. These 22 recent executions of juvenile offenders make up about 2% of the total executions since 1976[105]. These American juvenile executions were well based upon English practice. For example on Monday 12th of March 1716 William Jennings, age 12, was hanged at Tyburn, England, for housebreaking. On Saturday 18th March 1738, sixteen year old Mary Grote was tied a hurdle and drawn along in a procession behind a cart, was chained to a large wooden stake, and bundles of faggots placed round her. The executioner may have strangled her with a rope before igniting the fire and reducing the girl to ashes. Mary had been convicted of the petty treason and murder of her mistress, Justine Turner. The common law at the time set the incapacity to commit a felony at age 14.

George Stinney Jr, a black youngster, was the youngest person to be executed in the United States in the twentieth century when he was sent to the electric chair in 1944. Most researchers who have studied this case have agreed upon the following facts. On the afternoon of March 23, 1944, Betty June Binnicker, age 11, and Mary Emma Thames, age 7, did not

---

[103] Steinberg, Laurence & Scott, Elizabeth, "Less Guilty by Reason of Adolescence: Developmental Immaturity, Diminished Responsibility, and the Juvenile Death Penalty", *American Psychologist* 58: 1009.

[104] Erikson, Erik, *Identity, Youth and Crisis*. New York: Norton, 1968.

[105] "History of the Juvenile Death Penalty." *Washington Post*, 19 July 1988.

return to their homes in rural Alcolu, South Carolina. The next morning authorities launched a search for the missing children and quickly the searchers located their bodies lying in a ditch. In both cases the girls' skulls had been crushed and a bicycle lay on top of their bodies. George Stinney Jr. was taken into custody a few hours later, although it has never been established how police focused on this child. Police maintained that he confessed to murdering the girls within hours of his apprehension. While law enforcement testified that Stinney had made a full confession, no written confession has subsequently been located.

The boy's parents were threatened and were ordered to leave the city. Prior to his trial, George spent 81 days in detention without the possibility of seeing his parents for the last time. He was imprisoned alone in his cell, eighty kilometers from his hometown. The hearing of the facts was conducted with Stinney alone, without either the presence of his parents or a lawyer.

The defendant was tried for the murder of Betty June Binnicker on April 24, 1944, just one month after being taken into custody. The prosecution selected an all-white male jury and the trial was concluded that same day during a special term of court with Judge P. H. Stoll presiding. Appearing on behalf of the State was Solicitor Frank McLeod, who presented evidence from law enforcement that Stinney had confessed to the crime. Stinney did have a lawyer, Charles H. Plowden, but there is no evidence that he served his client in any meaningful way. Among other defects Plowden failed to challenge the selection of an all-white jury. He did not examine the law officers about the circumstances of the confession. He also failed to bring any witnesses or present any evidence on behalf of Stinney.

The trial lasted two hours and thirty minutes; the jury rendered its sentencing decision after deliberating 10 minutes. Reportedly, prosecution presented no evidence and offered only a small amount of witness testimonies. The 14-year-old child was sentenced to death for the murder of two white girls in a segregated mill town in South Carolina. From his trial to the execution room, it was reported that the boy always had his Bible in his hands while claiming his innocence. After the trial, Plowden opted to not appeal Stinney's conviction and especially the death sentence.[106]

On 6 June 1944 George Stinney, Jr., was executed at age fourteen years. A newspaper account of the execution read, "Young Stinney was such a small boy that it was difficult to adjust the electrode to his right leg. After the first charge of 2,400 volts was sent coursing through his body, the death mask slipped from his face and his eyes were open when two additional shots of 1,400 and 500 volts followed."[107]

More than 70 years after his death his conviction has been overturned. South Carolina Circuit Judge Carmen Mullen said the speed with which the state meted out justice against the boy was shocking and extremely unfair, and that his case was one of "great injustice" in her ruling exonerating Stinney Jr. Technically, Judge Mullen did not officially "recognize" Stinney's "innocence," but rather vacated his conviction on the basis that his trial and sentencing had violated his constitutional due process rights.[108]

The claim that Stinney was the youngest person to be executed in the United States in the twentieth century is probably accurate. Another black teenager, Fortune Ferguson, reportedly was 13 years old in 1923 when he was convicted and sentenced to death for the rape of an eight-year-old girl in Florida, but his execution, also carried out by electrocution, was stayed and delayed for four years. There is some question as to his real age at the time of his conviction. A 1924 newspaper article reported he was 17 years old, while a 1927 article said that he was 22 years old at the time of his execution.[109]

---

[106] "Young Negro Electrocuted for Double Murder." *Murfreesboro Daily News-Journal,* 16 June 1944; "Negro Youth, 14, Dies in Chair." *Tampa Bay Times,* 17 June 1944; "George Stinney, Who Killed Two Little Girls, Dies Calmly." *Greenville News*, 17 June 1944.

[107] *Columbia Record,* June 16, 1944.

[108] Santaella, Tony. "Judge Throws Out Black Teen's Conviction from 1944." *USA Today,* 17 December 2014.

[109] "Negro Is Executed After Long Fight." *Tampa Times*, 27 April 1927; "Negro Stoically Awaits His Death in State's Chair." *Orlando Sentinel,* 19 September 1924; "Negro Put to Death for Criminal Attack." *Tampa Tribune*, 28 April 1927. See also https:// www.snopes.com / fact-check / george – stinney - execution-exoneration/

In the 1978 companion cases of *Lockett v. Ohio* and *Bell v. Ohio*, the Supreme Court held that sentencing juries and judges must consider all mitigating factors offered by the defendant, including the defendant's age. In *Bell*, the defendant was not allowed to present his youth as a mitigating factor and was thereafter sentenced to death for a crime he committed at the age of sixteen. Because the Ohio statute narrowly limited the introduction of mitigating circumstances, the Court reversed the defendant's death sentence.[110]

In 1982, the Supreme Court, in Ed dings *v. Oklahoma*,[111] agreed to consider the constitutionality of the death penalty as applied to a sixteen-year-old offender. For whatever reasons the court did not rule on the legality of executing a minor of that tender age, but remanded it for re-sentencing along the lines required by the *Lockett* and *Bell* rulings.

## *Thompson v. Oklahoma*

On January 23, 1983 Tony Mann, Richard Jones, Bobby Glass and William Wayne Thompson kidnapped and killed Charles Kine. While trying to escape, Keene ran and knocked on the door of neighbor John Brown's door, screaming "they're going to kill me". When Brown opened the door he saw four men dragging Keene from his front door to their car all the while beating on him. Brown called the police but by the time they arrived the four men had already left. Keene was the husband of Thompson's sister Vicki. Reportedly, Keene was abusive to his wife and other family members. Two of the abductors were identified as her half-brother Tony Man, and her real brother William Thompson. When the kidnappers were captured they said that Vicki had complained so much that they felt it necessary to take action. At that time Oklahoma law allow murderers who are minors to be tried and punished as adults if they understood what they were doing was wrong. The law also required proof that "aggravating circumstances" were involved in the commission of a capital crime.[112]

Prosecution introduced to the court several gruesome photographs

---

[110] *Lockett v Ohio*, 438 U.S. 586 (1978); *Bell v Ohio,* 438 U.S. 637 (1978).

[111] *Eddings v. Oklahoma,* 455 U.S. 104 (1982).

[112] https://caselaw.findlaw.com/us-supreme-court/487/815.html

of the murder, showing the cruel nature of murder. Prosecutors claimed that Thompson was a genuine threat to society before this murder Thompson had been arrested on multiple occasions for assault, battery and attempted burglary. Mary Robinson, a social worker for the juvenile justice system, testified that counseling Thompson did not improve his behavior. The jury thus decided he would continue to be a threat to society and voted for the death sentence. The court of criminal appeals ruled in favor of Oklahoma, stating that if Thompson was old enough to commit murder, then he defiantly was old enough to be punished as an adult.[113]

The case came before the U. S. Supreme Court on appeal which ruled 5 to 3, that states may not execute people for crimes committed when they were less than 16 years old, at least not unless the concerned states adopted new legislation explicitly providing that people under 16 may be executed. A state that chooses to adopt new legislation specifying a minimum age for the death penalty can do so only after "careful consideration." The case had attracted great attention both nationally and internationally.

Four members of the Court joined in an opinion written by Justice John Paul Stevens that held that "evolving standards of decency" compelled the conclusion that it would be unconstitutional under any circumstances to execute a person for a crime committed as a 15-year-old. Justice John Paul Stevens's plurality opinion left open the possibility that the Court might later bar execution of anyone who was under 18 when the crime was committed. Justice John Paul Stevens said, "Executing people for childhood crimes is cruel and unusual punishment." Execution for this crime, Justice Stevens wrote, would be "nothing more than the purposeless and needless imposition of pain and suffering."

In the plurality opinion, Justice Stevens noted that the defendant's victim, Charles Keene, had been abducted, beaten and shot twice and his throat, chest and abdomen had been cut before his body was chained to a concrete block and thrown into a river.

Nonetheless, Justice Stevens ruled that execution of William

---

[113] 724 P.2d 780,

Wayne Thompson, the defendant.

Asserting that it was clear that, for example, a 10-year-old child could not constitutionally be executed, he said it was significant that none of the 18 states that have expressly considered and established a minimum age in their death-penalty laws allow execution for crimes committed under the of age 16.

Justice Stevens also noted that most other nations of the world, including the Soviet Union as well as most Western nations, prohibit "juvenile executions." "These indicators of contemporary standards of decency confirm our judgment that such a young person is not capable of acting with the degree of culpability that can justify the ultimate penalty," he said.

Justice Sandra Day O'Connor, the critical fifth vote to spare the defendant's life, said she would not go as far as Justice Stevens. But she held that that states may not execute persons for crimes committed at age 15 or younger "under the authority of a capital punishment statute that specifies no minimum age." She noted that "no legislature in this country has affirmatively and unequivocally endorsed" capital punishment for 15-year-olds, although nineteen states "authorize capital punishment without setting any statutory minimum age." That consideration Justice O'Connor found wanting in the Oklahoma law.

Justice Antonin Scalia dissented, in the case, joined by Chief Justice William H. Rehnquist and Justice Byron R. White. In his dissent, Justice Scalia said that the Court should not rule as it did today unless there was a "national consensus that no criminal so much as one day under 16" could ever "possibly be deemed mature and responsible enough to be punished with death for any crime." He said there was no such consensus. Moreover, he said the Eighth Amendment's ban on "cruel and unusual punishments" was not originally intended to ban execution of juveniles and "limits the evolving standards appropriate for our consideration to those entertained by the society rather than those dictated by our personal consciences."[114]

---

[114] Simmons, Susan M. "Thompson v. Oklahoma: Debating the Constitutionality of Juvenile Executions," 16 *Pepp. L. Rev.* 3 (1989)

Justice Anthony M. Kennedy, who joined the Court after the November 9 oral argument, did not participate.[115]

## *Stanford v. Kentucky*

In 1989, the United States Supreme Court held that the Eighth Amendment does not prohibit the death penalty for crimes committed at ages 16 or 17.[116] Kevin Stanford, aged 17 years and 4 months, murdered Barbel Poore in Jefferson County, Kentucky on January 7, 1981. Stanford and his accomplice repeatedly raped and sodomized Ms. Poore during and after their commission of a robbery at a gas station. Stanford shot Ms. Poore pointblank in the face and then in the back of her head. A Kentucky juvenile court conducted hearings to determine whether he should be transferred for trial as an adult. That relevant statute provided that juvenile court jurisdiction could be waived and an offender tried as an adult if he was either charged with a Class A felony or capital crime, or was over 16 years of age and charged with a felony. The juvenile court certified Stanford for trial as an adult, holding that this was in the best interest of petitioner and the community.[117]

Stanford was convicted of murder, first-degree sodomy, first-degree robbery and receiving stolen property, and was sentenced to death. Stanford was convicted of murder, first-degree sodomy, first-degree robbery and receiving stolen property, and was sentenced to death. The Kentucky Supreme Court affirmed the death sentence, rejecting Stanford's "deman[d] that he has a constitutional right to treatment." Finding that the record clearly demonstrated that "there was no program or treatment appropriate for the appellant in the juvenile justice system," the court held that the juvenile court did not err in certifying Stanford for trial as an adult.

---

[115] *Thompson v. Oklahoma*, 487 U.S. 815 (1988)

[116] *Stanford v. Kentucky* (1989)

[117] *Stanford v. Commonwealth*, 734 S.W.2d 781, 792 (Ky. 1987), afj'd sub nom. *Stanford v. Kentucky,* 109 S. Ct. 2969 (1989). Petitioner Stanford had been in and out of juvenile court and treatment programs since the age of 10. Efforts at rehabilitation were obviously unsuccessful. The court reasoned that resubjecting Stanford to unproductive therapy only to return him to the streets to continue the pattern of crime would be contrary to the interests of the community and of petitioner himself.

The court also stated that Stanford's "age and the possibility that he might be rehabilitated were mitigating factors appropriately left to the consideration of the jury that tried him."

While considering Stanford's appeal the Supreme Court also heard a parallel case from the State of Missouri.[118] The Supreme Court affirmed the verdicts of capital punishment in both cases handed down in lower courts. Justice Antonin Scalia wrote the Opinion of the Court. He noted that neither Stanford nor Wilkins had asserted that the punishment was cruel or unusual at the time the Bill of Rights was adopted. Thus, both petitioners were left to argue that capital punishment for minors older than the common law age of 14, was contrary to "the evolving standards of decency."[119] Justice Scalia wrote,

> We discern neither a historical nor a modern societal consensus forbidding the imposition of capital punishment on any person who murders at 16 or 17 years of age. Accordingly, we conclude that such punishment does not offend the Eighth Amendment's prohibition against cruel and unusual punishment. . . . and to mean that as the dissent means it, i.e., that it is for us to judge, not on the basis of what we perceive the Eighth Amendment originally prohibited, or on the basis of what we perceive the society through its democratic processes now overwhelmingly disapproves, but on the basis of what we think "proportionate" and "measurably contributory to acceptable goals of punishment" -- to say and mean that, is to replace judges of the law with a committee of philosopher-kings.

Justice Sandra Day O'Connor, agreed that no national consensus forbade the imposition of capital punishment on 16- or 17-year-old murderers. She concluded that the court has a constitutional obligation to conduct proportionality analysis, and should consider age-based statutory classifications that are relevant to that analysis. Justice Brennan filed a

---

[118] *Wilkins v. Missouri,* 487 U.S. 1233 (1988).

[119] Dalton, Laura. "Stanford v. Kentucky and Wilkins v. Missouri: A Violation of an Emerging Rule of Customary International Law," 32 *Wm. & Mary L. Rev.* 161 (1990).

dissenting opinion, in which he was joined by Justices Marshall, Blackmun, and Stevens.[120]

## *Woodson v. North Carolina*

Petitioners were convicted of first-degree murder as the result of their participation in an armed robbery of a convenience food store where the cashier was killed and a customer was seriously wounded. The Supreme Court of North Carolina upheld their sentences under the new North Carolina statute, which required death sentences for all defendants convicted of that crime. Upon appeal to the U.S. Supreme Court *Certiorari* was granted challenging the constitutionality of the statute. The high court was asked to decide whether the North Carolina's statute imposing mandatory death sentence for a first-degree murder violate the Eighth and Fourteenth Amendments.

The Court concluded that mandatory death penalties are incompatible with contemporary values and cannot be applied in consistency with requirement that the State's power to punish "be exercised within the limits of civilized standards." Writing for the court, Justice Stewart penned "The belief no longer prevails that every offense in a like legal category calls for an identical punishment without regard to the past life and habits of a particular offender,"[121]

The court found another deficiency of North Carolina's mandatory death sentence statute: it failed to respond to *Furman v. Georgia*. Justice Stewart wrote, "The North Carolina statute fails to provide a constitutionally tolerable response to Furman's rejection of unbridled jury discretion in the imposition of capital sentences. Central to the limited holding in that case was the conviction that vesting a jury with standard-less sentencing power violated the Eighth and Fourteenth Amendments, yet that constitutional deficiency is not eliminated by the mere formal removal of all sentencing power from juries in capital cases. In view of the historic record, it may reasonably be assumed that many juries under mandatory statutes will continue to consider the grave consequences of a conviction in reaching verdict. But the North Carolina statute provides no

---

[120] *Stanford v. Kentucky*, 492 U.S. 361 (1989)
[121] Citing *Williams v. New York*, 337 U. S. 241, 337 U. S. 247.

standards to guide the jury in determining which murderers shall live and which shall die."[122]

The court also held that the Eight Amendment requires consideration of various aspects of the character of the individual offender and the circumstances of the particular offense as a "constitutionally indispensable part of the process of imposing the ultimate punishment of death". The North Carolina statute did not allow such a particularized approach.

Thus, the U.S. Supreme Court found that the North Carolina mandatory death penalty statute is in violation of the Eighth and Fourteenth Amendments and must be set aside.[123] Justice Stewart wrote the opinion of the court joined by Justices Powell, Stevens and Brennan. Justice Marshall again announced his total opposition to the death sentence. Justice White dissented joined by Justices Rehnquist and Burger.

Christopher Simmons, age 17, committed murder. About nine months later, after he had turned 18, he was tried and sentenced to death. There is essentially no doubt that Simmons was the instigator of the crime for Simmons had earlier said he wanted to murder someone. In chilling, callous terms he talked about his plan, discussing it with two friends, Charles Benjamin and John Tessmer, then aged 15 and 16 respectively. Simmons proposed to commit burglary and murder by breaking and entering, tying up a victim, and throwing the victim off a bridge. Simmons assured his friends they could "get away with it" because they were minors.

The three met at about 2 a.m. on the night of the murder, but Tessmer left before the other two set out. The State later charged Tessmer with conspiracy, but dropped the charge in exchange for his testimony against Simmons. He knew Mrs. Shirley Crook from an earlier automobile accident. He later admitted that this fact had confirmed his resolve to murder her. Simmons and Benjamin entered the home of the victim, Mrs. Shirley Crook, and Simmons turned on a hallway light. Awakened, Mrs. Crook called out, asking "Who's there?" In response Simmons entered Mrs. Crook's bedroom. Using duct tape to cover her eyes and mouth and

---

[122] *Woodson v. North Carolina*, 428 U.S. 280 at 302-03 (1976)
[123] *Woodson v. North Carolina*, 428 U.S. 280 (1976)

bind her hands, the two perpetrators put Mrs. Crook in her minivan and drove to a state park. They reinforced the bindings, covered her head with a towel, and walked her to a railroad trestle spanning the Meramec River. There they tied her hands and feet together with electrical wire, wrapped her whole face in duct tape and threw her from the bridge, drowning her in the waters below.

On September 9, the husband Steven Crook had returned home from an overnight trip, found his bedroom in disarray, and reported his wife missing. On the same afternoon fishermen recovered the victim's body from the river. Simmons, meanwhile, was bragging about the killing, telling friends he had killed a woman. The next day, having received information of Simmons' involvement, police arrested him at his high school and took him to the police station in Fenton, Missouri, where they read him his *Miranda* rights. Simmons waived his right to an attorney and agreed to answer questions. After less than two hours of interrogation, Simmons confessed to the murder and agreed to perform a videotaped reenactment at the crime scene.

The State charged Simmons with burglary, kidnapping, stealing, and murder in the first degree. He was tried as an adult. At trial the State introduced Simmons' confession and the videotaped reenactment of the crime, along with testimony that Simmons discussed the crime in advance and bragged about it later. The defense called no witnesses in the guilt phase. The jury returned a verdict of murder so the trial proceeded to the penalty phase. The State sought the death penalty. As aggravating factors, the State submitted that the murder was committed for the purpose of receiving money; was committed for the purpose of avoiding, interfering with, or preventing lawful arrest of the defendant; and involved depravity of mind and was outrageously and wantonly vile, horrible, and inhuman. The State called Shirley Crook's husband, daughter, and two sisters, who presented moving evidence of the devastation her death had brought to their lives

As a mitigating factor Simmons' attorneys first called an officer of the Missouri juvenile justice system, who testified that Simmons had no prior convictions and that no previous charges had been filed against him. Simmons' mother, father, two younger half-brothers, a neighbor, and a friend took the stand to tell the jurors of the close relationships they had formed with Simmons and to plead for mercy on his behalf. The trial judge had instructed the jurors they could consider his age as a mitigating factor. Defense counsel reminded the jurors that juveniles of Simmons' age cannot drink, serve on juries, or even see certain movies, because the legislatures have wisely decided that individuals of a certain age aren't responsible enough. The jury recommended the death penalty after finding the State had proved each of the three aggravating factors submitted to it. Accepting the jury's recommendation, the trial judge imposed the death penalty.

Simmons then obtained new counsel, who moved in the trial court to set aside the conviction and sentence. It advanced the argument that Simmons had received ineffective assistance at trial. To support this contention, the new counsel called as witnesses Simmons' original trial attorney, and the clinical psychologists who had evaluated him. New counsel argued that Simmons was "very immature," "very impulsive," and "very susceptible to being manipulated or influenced." The experts testified about Simmons' background including a difficult home environment and dramatic changes in behavior, accompanied by poor school performance in adolescence. Simmons was absent from home for long periods, spending time using alcohol and drugs with other teenagers or young adults. Counsel argued that these matters should have been introduced in the sentencing proceeding.

The Missouri Supreme Court affirmed court found no constitutional violation by reason of ineffective assistance of counsel and denied the motion for post-conviction relief. In a consolidated appeal from Simmons' conviction and sentence, and from the denial of post-conviction relief.[124] The federal courts denied Simmons' petition for a writ of habeas corpus.[125]

Following these proceedings the U. S. Supreme Court held that

---

[124] *State v. Simmons*, 944 S. W. 2d 165, 169 (en banc), cert. denied, 522 U.S. 953 (1997)
[125] *Simmons v. Bowersox*, 235 F.3d 1124, 1127 (CA8), cert. denied, 534 U.S. 924 (2001).

the Eighth and Fourteenth Amendments prohibit the execution of a mentally retarded person.[126] Simmons filed a new petition for state post-conviction relief, arguing that the reasoning employed in *Atkins* would also establish the principle that the Constitution prohibits the execution of juveniles who were under 18 when the crime was committed. The Missouri Supreme Court agreed. Using this reasoning it set aside Simmons' death sentence and re-sentenced him to life imprisonment without eligibility for probation, parole, or release.[127] It held that since Stanford, "a national consensus has developed against the execution of juvenile offenders, as demonstrated by the fact that eighteen states now bar such executions for juveniles, that twelve other states bar executions altogether, that no state has lowered its age of execution below 18 since *Stanford,* that five states have legislatively or by case law raised or established the minimum age at 18, and that the imposition of the juvenile death penalty has become truly unusual over the last decade."[128]

The State of Missouri appealed the decision to the U.S. Supreme Court, which granted certiorari. This case was argued on October 13, 2004. The 1988 Supreme Court decision, *Thompson v. Oklahoma*, had barred execution of offenders under the age of 16. In 1989, another case, as we have seen, Stanford *v. Kentucky*, upheld the possibility of capital punishment for offenders who were 16 or 17 years old when they committed the capital offense. Under the "evolving standards of decency" test, the Court held that it was cruel and unusual punishment to execute a person who was under the age of 18 at the time of the murder.

Justice Kennedy wrote the opinion of the court in which he cited a body of sociological and scientific research that found that juveniles have a lack of maturity and sense of responsibility compared to adults. In support of the national consensus position, the Court noted that states were reducing the frequency by which they applied capital punishment to juvenile offenders. At the time of the decision, 20 states had the juvenile death penalty on the books, but only six states had executed prisoners since

---

[126] *Atkins v. Virginia*, 536 U.S. 304 (2002)
[127] *State ex rel. Simmons v. Roper*, 112 S. W. 3d 397 (2003) (*en banc*)
[128] 112 S. W. 3d, at 399.

1989 for crimes committed as juveniles. Only three states had done so since 1994: Oklahoma, Texas, and Virginia. Furthermore, five of the states that allowed the juvenile death penalty at the time of the 1989 case had since abolished it.

The Court also looked to practices in other countries to support the holding. Between 1990 and the time of the case, the court said, "only seven countries other than the United States had executed juvenile offenders . . . Iran, Pakistan, Saudi Arabia, Yemen, Nigeria, Congo, and China." Justice Kennedy noted that since 1990, each of those countries had either abolished the death penalty for juveniles or made public disavowal of the practice, and that the United States stood alone in allowing execution of juvenile offenders. Still, Saudi Arabia, Iran, Pakistan, and Yemen continued to execute juvenile offenders after 2005. The Court also noted that only the United States and Somalia had not ratified Article 37 of the United Nations Convention on the Rights of the Child, which expressly prohibits capital punishment for crimes committed by juveniles. We granted certiorari, and now affirm.[129]

Justice Scalia wrote the dissenting opinion in which he was joined by Chief Justice Rehnquist and Justice Thomas. Justice O'Connor also wrote a dissenting opinion. The dissents put into question whether a "national consensus" had formed among the state laws, citing the fact that at the time of the ruling, only 18 of the 38 states allowing the death penalty (47%) prohibited the execution of juveniles.

However, the primary objection of Justices Scalia and Thomas, was whether such a consensus was relevant. Justice Scalia argued that the appropriate question was not whether there was presently a consensus against the execution of juveniles, but rather whether the execution of such defendants was considered cruel and unusual at the point at which the Bill of Rights was ratified. In addition, Justice Scalia also objected in general to the Court's willingness to take guidance from foreign law in interpreting the Constitution; his dissent questioned not only the relevance of foreign law but also claimed the Court would "invoke alien law when it agrees with one's own thinking, and ignore it otherwise," noting that in the case

---

[129] 540 U.S. 1160 (2004)

of abortion, U.S. laws are less restrictive than the international norm.

Justice Scalia also attacked the majority opinion as being fundamentally antidemocratic. His dissent cited a passage from *The Federalist Papers* in arguing that the role of the judiciary in the constitutional scheme is to interpret the law as formulated in democratically selected legislatures. He argued that the Court exists to rule on what the law says, not what it should say, and that it is for the legislature, acting in the manner prescribed in Article V of the Constitution to offer amendments to the Constitution in light of the evolving standard of decency, not for the Court to arbitrarily make de facto amendments. He challenged the right of unelected lawyers to discern moral values and to impose them on the people in the name of flexible readings of the constitutional text.[130]

## Gary Graham

Bobby Grant Lambert, a 53-year-old white resident of Tucson, Arizona, was visiting Houston, Texas in May 1981. He was staying at a nearby motel, but had checked out shortly before his trip to the grocery store. At approximately 9:30 p.m., on 13 May, Mr. Lambert was walking out of a Safeway supermarket in Houston, Texas, when an assailant approached Lambert and put his hand into Lambert's rear pocket. When Mr. Lambert resisted, the assailant pulled out a .22 caliber pistol and held it to Lambert's head. Mr. Lambert dropped his groceries as the assailant shot him in the chest. As the assailant fled, Lambert stumbled back into the grocery store, where he died. The robber got away with the change from a $100 bill, although police later found $6000 in $100 bills on the victim's body.

A week later on May 20, 1981, Gary Graham, a 5'10" black 17-year-old resident of Houston, abducted Lisa Blackburn, a 57-year-old taxi driver at a gas station, took her to a vacant lot and raped her. He then went to her house, where he collected her valuables, but then fell asleep. Blackburn confiscated his gun and his clothes, and called the police. When the police arrived, they arrested Graham for her rape and abduction.

---

[130] *Roper v. Simmons*, 543 U.S. 551 (2005)

Upon further examination they linked Graham to 22 crimes that had occurred between May 13 and May 20. Because Graham's crimes were robberies committed with a .22 caliber handgun, police included Graham's arrest photo in the photo array shown to witnesses in the Bobby Lambert murder. Bernadine Skillern was a 45-year-old black Houston school district clerk who was sitting in her car in the Safeway parking lot the night of the murder.

On May 26, 1981, after describing the perpetrator to the police, Ms. Skillern picked Graham's mug shot from a photo spread. The following day, she again identified him as the murderer in a lineup. Skillern described the perpetrator as a black male, between 18 and 20 years old, 5'10" to 6 feet tall, with slim build and a slim face that was clean-shaven with a close cut Afro hair-style. He was wearing a white jacket and black slacks and was carrying a black gun with a long barrel. She told the police that she saw a man put a pistol to Lambert's head. When she blew her horn, the gunman turned to look at her. She heard a popping sound; Lambert dropped his bag of groceries, and the other man fled. She followed the suspect in her car until her screaming children made her stop. She said that she got a good look at the killer for about a minute and a half through the windshield of her car, which was 20 to 30 feet away from the murder.

After the witness identified him as the gunman, Graham was charged with capital murder. He admitted to the crime spree and pled guilty to 10 cases of aggravated robbery and also the rape of 57-Ms Blackburn and faced 20-year prison sentences. He pled not guilty to the murder of Bobby Lambert. In October 1981, Graham was convicted of capital murder and sentenced to death. The Court of Criminal Appeals affirmed Graham's conviction and sentence and the convicting district court set Graham's execution for July 1987.[131]

Graham unsuccessfully brought a series of state *habeas corpus* proceedings on several grounds, including a claim of actual innocence, and the Court of Criminal Appeals denied relief on each occasion. Graham also brought an unsuccessful federal *habeas corpus* petition arguing that the

---

[131] *Graham v. State,* 671 S.W.2d 529 (Tex. Crim. App. 1984).

statutory special issues used in his sentencing were unconstitutional because they failed to allow full consideration of his mitigating evidence. After Graham had been denied relief on these challenges, the convicting court reset Graham's execution for April 29, 1993. Graham then sought habeas corpus relief in federal court a second time, based in part on his claim of actual innocence supported by newly discovered evidence. The major defense objection of course was Graham's age.[132]

He became a political activist and in 1995 changed his name from Gary Lee Graham to Shaka Sankofa. When all appeals had failed prison authorities took no chances at the execution. Police separated Graham's opponents and supporters to opposite ends of the prison. At one point, about a hundred Graham supporters attempted to confront around twenty Ku Klux Klansmen demonstrating in favor of the execution, but the police kept them apart. Sankofa resisted when the time came for him to be taken to the death chamber. A prison team had to be dispatched to force him towards the death chamber. It took five jail guards to strap him to the gurney. He was executed by lethal injection on June 22, 2000 in Huntsville, Texas.[133]

---

[132] *Ex parte Graham,* 853 S.W.2d 565, 566 (Tex. Crim. App.), cert. denied sub nom. *Graham v. Texas*, 113 S. Ct. 2431 (1993) detailing Graham's state habeas corpus challenges.

[133] "Gary Graham" in Wikipedia; https://capitalpunishmentincontext.org/issues/juveniles

# Insanity

When the Supreme Court ruled in 2002 [134] that executing defendants with mental retardation was unconstitutional, it did not address the constitutionality of executing persons with mental illness. Mental illness differs from intellectual disability. [135] Intellectual disability is measured by subnormal intellectual development with various cognitive deficiencies, usually appearing at an early age. The National Alliance on Mental Illness defines mental illnesses as "medical conditions that disrupt a person's thinking, feeling, mood, ability to relate to others and daily functioning." Many death row inmates suffer from mental illnesses, including schizophrenia, bipolar disorder, delusions, and other impairments. Some were mentally ill before the crime for which they were convicted and for others the mental illness developed or worsened in prison.

Most of what was known and practiced in the early history of the United States was based upon English practice and experience. Prior to 1700 there was no clear understanding of mental illness and how insanity should be handled in the courts.

In 1986 in *Ford v Wainwright* the U. S. Supreme Court noted that English antecedents regarding execution of the insane: "Sir Edward Coke had earlier expressed the same view of the common law of England: "[B]y intendment of Law the execution of the offender is for example, . . . but so it is not when a mad man is executed, but should be a miserable spectacle,

---

[134] *Atkins v. Virginia*, 536 U.S. 304 (2002).
[135] Also known as mental retardation

both against Law, and of extreme inhumanity and cruelty, and can be no example to others."[136] Other recorders of the common law concurred. See 1 M. Hale, *Pleas of the Crown* 35 (1736); 1 W. Hawkins, *Pleas of the Crown* 2 (7th ed. 1795); Hawles, *Remarks on the Trial of Mr. Charles Bateman*, 11 How. St. Tr. 474, 477 (1685)."

One of the earliest recorded cases of insanity being used a defense was an English trial, *Rex v Arnold*, decided in 1724. Edward Arnold was tried at Kingston, Surrey for shooting at Lord Onslow. Arnold claimed that t he had done so was because Onslow had bewitched him and had sent into his bed-chamber "devils and imps", that had "invaded his bosom such that he could not sleep." Arnold's relatives testified that he suffered from delusions. Trial judge Justice Tracy instructed the jury that to acquit they had to decide whether the accused was totally deprived of his understanding and memory and knew what he was doing "no more than a wild beast or a brute, or an infant". This instruction became known as "the wild-beast test." The jury found Arnold to be sane convicted and sentenced him to death but was reprieved at the urging of his victim.

In England again in1760 Lawrence Shirley, the 4th Earl Ferrers was convicted of the murder of John Johnson, his estate steward. At his trial he attempted to use a defence of insanity. In trial many acquaintances who knew him thought him to be insane and so testified. The prosecution pointed out to the court that Ferrers should be found guilty unless it could be shown that he did not possess sufficient mental capacity to understand the consequences of his action. Jurors accepted this concept and so Ferrers was executed.

In 1800 England tried one James Hadfield for treason for having shot at the King George III. The charge was treason, a capital offense and Hadfield employed defense counsel Thomas Erskine. As a treason case the matter was heard by the Lord Chief Justice. Erskine challenged the prevailing legal definition of insanity, telling the court that a person could "know what he was about", but be unable to resist his "delusion." Dr. John Monro of Bedlam Hospital examined Hadfield and determined that he suffered from delusions, most probably brought on by serious head injuries

---

[136] Coke, Edward. *Institutes* 3: 6 (6th ed. 1680)

received during the war with France in 1794. Erskine told the court that Hadfield believed that God talked to him all the time and had told him that the world was about to end. The defense proved successful and Hadfield was sent to Britain's first mental hospital.

The Hadfield case led to the passage of the Criminal Lunatics Act of 1800 which provided that "in all cases where it shall be given in evidence upon the trial of any person charged with treason, murder, or felony, that such person was insane at the time of the commission of such offense, and such person shall be acquitted, the jury shall be required to find specially whether such person was insane at the time of the commission of such offense, and to declare whether such person was acquitted by them on account of such insanity; and if they shall find that such person was insane at the time of the committing such offense, the court before whom such trial shall be had, shall order such person to be kept in strict custody, in such place and in such manner as to the court shall seem fit, until His Majesty's pleasure shall be known.[137]"

The landmark case that was to shape the future of the legal definition of insanity for well over a century was that of Daniel M'Naughten.[138] That man killed Edward Drummond in 1843. The intended victim was again the Prime Minister, but M'Naughten mistook Drummond for the Prime Minister and as he left Peel's house, followed him and shot him in the back with a single round. M'Naughten was arrested at the scene before he could fire again. He believed that Peel and others were watching his every move and conspiring against him to destroy him. The crown brought M'Naughten to trial and presented evidence of his insanity. His father told them that his son had suffered from delusions of persecution as a teenager. While awaiting trial various physicians examined M'Naughten. The physicians specialized in treating lunatics, as they were then known. Universally they testified to M'Naughten's insanity and delusional behaviour. One physician introduced the relatively new concept of monomania, testifying that the

---

[137] "Insanity and the Death Penalty" http://www.capitalpunishmentuk.org/insanity.html
[138] *M'Naghten's Case* [1843] All ER Rep 229

delusions "operated to the extent of depriving M'Naughten of all self-control." Mr. Justice Tindal told the jury "the question to be determined is, whether at the time the act in question was committed, the prisoner had or had not the use of his understanding, so as to know that he was doing a wrong or wicked act." The jury found in his favour and M'Naughten was committed to the Bedlam Hospital for the Insane. The verdict caused considerable public consternation, so the House of Lords in March 1843 formulated the famous M'Naughten Rules which state that : "Every man is to be presumed to be sane, and ... that to establish a defense on the ground of insanity, it must be clearly proved that, at the time of the committing of the act, the party accused was laboring under such a defect of reason, from disease of mind, and not to know the nature and quality of the act he was doing; or if he did know it, that he did not know he was doing what was wrong."[139]

A finding of insanity will likely result in indefinite confinement in a hospital, whereas a conviction for murder might result in a determinate sentence of between ten and fifteen years. Faced with this choice, it may well be that defendants would prefer the latter option. Even though a legal definition suffices, mandatory hospitalisation can be ordered in cases of murder but if the defendant is not medically insane, there is little point in requiring medical treatment. Diabetes has been held to facilitate a defence of insanity when it causes hyperglycaemia, but not when it causes hypoglycaemia.

## John Haggerty, 1846

John Haggerty was an Irishman who would frequently go mad from drinking too much. He had earlier attempted to kill one Sebastian Wise previously while drunk. For that attack he was sentenced to two years imprisonment. During a fit in which he thought his horse an evil spirit, he killed it with a silver bullet. Haggerty reported that another horse tried to climb a light pole.

Haggerty lived on South Queen Street, Lancaster, Pennsylvania,

---

[139] Kaplan, John, and Robert Weisberg. *Criminal Law: Cases and Materials*. 2d ed. Boston: Little, Brown, 1991; also Elliott, Carl. *The Rules of Insanity: Moral Responsibility and the Mentally Ill Offender*. SUNY Press, 1996.

near Melchior Fordney's gun shop. On 18 October 1846, in a highly
inebriated state, Haggerty secured a gun and attempted to shoot a certain
Mr. Funk. When the gun misfired he tried again, this time killing a horse.
He then took an axe and murdered Melchior Fordney (1781-1846) and the
Catherine Tipple, the woman with whom Fordney lived, and their child.
He struck a baby, knocking out some of its brains and partially
dismembering it. A son, aged about 12, got away through a window and
summoned police. When a neighbor named Steigerwalt arrived Haggerty
was still wielding the axe against the three dead bodies and attempted to
attack Steigerwalt. Member of a crowd which had gathered felled
Haggerty with a hail of stones.[140]

Melchior Fordney had married Mary Michel in 1804, but theirs
was not a happy union and he moved out and started a second family.
Haggerty claimed that Fordney was committing adultery and thus living
in great sin. He committed the murder to expiate that sin.

The court assembled a panel of eminent local physicians who
examined Haggerty. Psychiatry was not yet a medical specialty, but the
physicians did their best to determine whether or not Haggerty was
sufficiently sane to stand trial. The finally decided that only acceptable
diagnosis was the legal definition, that Haggerty was capable of
distinguishing between right and wrong. He was sentenced to be
hanged"[141] Reportedly, this was the first attempt to determine sanity in a
capital case in the United States through medical diagnosis.

The local newspaper reported Haggerty's execution. "John
Haggerty was executed to-day for the murder of the Melchior Fordney
family. He prayed with his religious advisers, Rev. Messrs. Keenan and

---

[140] Lancaster *Democratic Banner*, 30 October 1846. See also *The Peoples
Advocate*, 29 October 1846.

[141] *Report of the Trial and Conviction of John Haggerty for the murder of
Melchior Fordney, Late of the City of Lancaster, Pennsylvania: in the Court
of Oyer & Terminer, Held at the City of Lancaster, for the County of Lancaster,
at January term, A.D. 1847. Before the Hon. Ellis Lewis, President and Jacob
Grosh and Emanuel Schaeffer Associate Justices of Said Court. Lancaster,*
1847. 82 pp. This was largely a compilation of reports from Lancaster
newspapers. It did detail the examination and reasoning of the panel of
physicians.

Mayer. The drop fell at 10 hours, 14 minutes, A. M., and he was cut down at 1 hour, 30 minutes, P. M."[142]

## *Ford v. Wainwright*

In 1974, a Florida court sentenced Alvin Bernard Ford to death for first-degree murder of a Florida police officer. At the time of the murder, trial, and sentencing phase, there was no indication that Ford was suffering from any mental deficiencies. While awaiting execution, Ford's mental condition worsened. In early 1982 Ford began to manifest changes in behavior, becoming more serious over time. After reading in the newspaper that the Ku Klux Klan had held a rally in nearby Jacksonville, Florida, Ford developed an obsession focused upon the Klan. He displayed an increasingly pervasive delusion that he had become the target of a complex conspiracy, involving the Klan. He believed that the prison guards, part of the conspiracy, had been killing people and putting the bodies in the concrete enclosures used for beds. Later, he began to believe that his women relatives were being tortured and sexually abused somewhere in the prison. This notion developed into a delusion that the people who were tormenting him at the prison had taken members of Ford's family hostage. He began to refer to himself as "Pope John Paul, III," and reported that he had some appointed nine new justices to the Florida State Supreme Court.

Counsel for Ford asked a psychiatrist, Dr. Jamal Amin, to continue seeing him and to recommend appropriate treatment. On the basis of roughly 14 months of evaluation, Dr. Amin concluded in 1983 that Ford suffered from "a severe, uncontrollable, mental disease which closely resembles "Paranoid Schizophrenia With Suicide Potential".[143]

His competency was assessed in accordance with Florida procedures. Following this assessment, Florida's Governor signed Ford's death warrant. A state court declined to hear arguments raised about Ford's

---

[142] *Daily Morning Post*, 24 July 1847. *The Huntingdon Journal* of 3 August 1847 made the same report, adding that Haggerty was calm, even stoic, as death approached.

[143] Miller, Kent S. and Radelet, Michael L. *Executing the Mentally Ill: The Criminal Justice System and the Case of Alvin Ford*. London: Sage, 1993.

competency.[144] Without the benefit of a hearing, Ford's habeas corpus petition was then denied by the federal district court. The U.S. Court of Appeals for the Eleventh Circuit affirmed.

The question the Supreme Court had to answer was: Does the cruel and unusual punishment clause of the Eighth Amendment and the due process clause of the Fourteenth Amendment prohibit the imposition of the death penalty upon the insane? In a 7-2 decision, Justice Thurgood Marshall writing for the majority noted that English common law found executing the insane "savage and inhumane." In addition, no State permitted such executions. Such an execution "offends humanity. Moreover, such executions had neither a deterrent nor a retributive effect. On the second question, Marshall observed that no state court had heard arguments that Ford was insane. In addition, Florida's competency procedures were inadequate.[145]

Concurring, Justice Lewis F. Powell agreed that executing an insane inmate violated the Eighth Amendment. For Powell, "the Eighth Amendment forbids the execution only of those who are unaware of the punishment they are about to suffer and why they are to suffer it." Powell also argued that Florida's procedure for determining the competency of the inmate violated due process.

Justice Sandra Day O'Connor joined by Justice Byron R. White, dissented in part. They agreed that Florida's procedures did not protect Ford's due process rights. Justice O'Connor wrote, "I am in full agreement with Justice Rehnquist's conclusion that the Eighth Amendment does not create a substantive right not to be executed while insane. Accordingly, I do not join the Court's reasoning or opinion. Because, however, the conclusion is for me inescapable that Florida positive law has created a protected liberty interest in avoiding execution while incompetent, and because Florida does not provide even those minimal procedural protections required by due process in this area, I would vacate the judgment and remand to the Court of Appeals with directions that the case

---

[144] *Ford v. Wainwright*, 451 So.2d 471 (Fla. 1984).
[145] Miller, Kent S. and Radelet, Michael L. *Executing the Mentally Ill: The Criminal Justice System and the Case of Alvin Ford*. London: Sage, 199

be returned to the Florida system so that a hearing can be held in a manner consistent with the requirements of the Due Process Clause. I cannot agree, however, that the federal courts should have any role whatever in the substantive determination of a defendant's competency to be executed."

Justice William H. Rehnquist further, joined by Chief Justice Warren E. Burger, also maintained that no substantive right was created. In addition, Justice Rehnquist argued that the State's procedures drew sustenance from the common law and were not out of step with contemporary practice.[146]

Florida transferred Alvin Ford to the Florida State Hospital for treatment and evaluation. After he was reevaluated he was found to be incompetent to be executed.

## *Singleton v. Norris*

On 1 June 1979 Charles Laverne Singleton murdered Mary Lou York murdered during a robbery in York's Grocery Store at Hamburg. She died from loss of blood as a result of two stab wounds in her neck. The evidence of guilt in this case is overwhelming. Patti Franklin saw her relative Singleton enter York's Grocery at approximately 7:30 p.m. on the day of the crime. Shortly after Singleton entered Patti heard Mrs. York scream, asking Patti to get help, noting that "Charles Singleton is killing me." Another witness, Lenora Howard, observed Singleton exit the store and shortly thereafter witnessed Mrs. York, who was crying and had blood on her, come to the front door. Police Officer Strother was the first to arrive at the scene and found Mrs. York lying in a pool of blood in the rear of the store. The officer testified Mrs. York told him that Charles Singleton came in the store, explained that he was robbing the store, grabbed her around the neck, and then stabbed her. She then told Officer Strother that she was dying. While en route to the hospital, she told Dr. J. D. Rankin several times that she was dying and that Singleton did it. Mrs. York did die before reaching the emergency room of the hospital.[147]

In 1979, the State of Arkansas convicted Singleton of capital

---

[146] *Ford v. Wainwright*, 477 U.S. 399 (1986).
[147] *Singleton v. State*, 623 S.W.2d 180 (Ark. 1981)

felony murder and aggravated robbery for which he received a sentence of death. The Arkansas Supreme Court upheld the sentence of death for the murder on direct appeal, but set aside a second charge, that of aggravated robbery. His execution was scheduled for June 4, 1982.[148]

Singleton's mental health began to deteriorate in 1987. He said he believed his prison cell was possessed by demons and that a prison doctor had implanted a device in his ear. In December 2001, he wrote to the appeals court to inform it that he did not believe his victim was dead and that she was "somewhere on earth waiting for me -- her groom." Based on extensive medical evaluations describing him as psychotic, his lawyers have argued that he was mentally incompetent and thus cannot be executed. Administration of certain drugs alleviated his symptoms.

Singleton then appealed to the federal courts for a stay of execution and writ of habeas corpus, raising claims including ineffective assistance of counsel, use of invalid aggravating factors, and that he was incompetent and thus ineligible for execution.[149] The federal appeals court in St. Louis ruled yesterday that officials in Arkansas can force a prisoner on death row to take anti-psychotic medication to make him sane enough to execute. Without the drugs, the prisoner, Singleton, could not be put to death under a United States Supreme Court decision that prohibits the execution of the insane. The Supreme Court has not ruled on whether prisoners may be medicated in order to make them competent to be executed.[150]

Over the years, Singleton had sometimes taken anti-psychotic medication voluntarily, but on other occasions had been forced to take it. Arkansas officials argued that Mr. Singleton must be medicated because he posed a danger to himself and to others. Singleton's lawyers responded

---

[148] *Singleton v. State,* 274 Ark. 126, 623 S.W.2d 180, (1981).

[149] Citing *Ford v. Wainwright,* 477 U.S. 399, 106 S.Ct. 2595, 91 L.Ed.2d 335 (1986)

[150] The Supreme Court has held that prisoners may be forced to take anti psychotic medications in some situations. Prisoners who are forced to take medications to ensure that they are competent to stand trial are entitled to a hearing to consider the medical appropriateness of the treatment, the risk the defendant poses to himself and others, and the drug's effect on the defendant's appearance, testimony and communications with his lawyer.

by saying that forcible medication "becomes illegal once an execution date is set because it is no longer in his best medical interests." The apparently applicable guidelines issued by the American Medical Association would prohibit giving medical treatment in order to make people competent to be executed.

The 6-to-5 decision was the first by a federal appeals court to allow such an execution. "Singleton presents the court with a choice between involuntary medication followed by an execution and no medication followed by psychosis and imprisonment," Judge Roger L. Wollman wrote for the majority in ruling by the United States Court of Appeals for the Eighth Circuit.[151]

Judge Wollman said the first choice was the better one, at least when the drugs were generally beneficial to the prisoner. He said courts did not need to consider the ultimate result of medicating the prisoner." Judges Wollman and Heaney differed yesterday on whether they rendered Singleton sane or merely masked his psychosis. Eligibility for execution is the only unwanted consequence of the medication," he wrote.

Judge Gerald W. Heaney, in dissent, said there was a third choice. He would have allowed Singleton to be medicated without fear of execution. "I believe," he wrote, "that to execute a man who is severely deranged without treatment, and arguably incompetent when treated, is the pinnacle of what Justice Marshall called 'the barbarity of exacting mindless vengeance.' "Judge Heaney added that the majority's holding presented physicians with an impossible ethical choice. Judge Heaney's opinion was joined by three other judges. Judge Diana Murphy dissented on a different ground. She said the record was not clear on whether Singleton was psychotic and that it was premature to take up the case.[152]

Singleton was forcibly medicated to make him sane enough for execution. Charles Singleton was executed on January 6, 2004 in Arkansas.[153]

---

[151] *Singleton v. Lockhart*, 653 F.Supp. 1114, 1116 (E.D.Ark. 1986).
[152] *Singleton v Norris,* 319 F.3d 1018 (2003). See also Liptak, Adam. "State Can Make Inmate Sane Enough to Execute" *New York Times*, 11 February 2003.
[153] Stone, Alan. "Condemned Prisoner Treated and Executed," *Psychiatric Times*,

## *Panetti v. Quarterman*

Six years before he shaved his head, donned camouflage fatigues, and fatally shot his in-laws in front of his estranged wife and daughter, Scott Panetti piled up furniture and valuables in his yard in Fredericksburg, Texas, and sprayed it all down with water to get rid of the devil he was sure had possessed the house. This was not the first time he had done something truly bizarre. As early as his 20s, Panetti had been diagnosed with paranoid schizophrenia, delusions, auditory hallucinations, and manic depression He had been hospitalized at least 14 times. Two years prior to the murders, he was involuntarily committed after swinging a cavalry sword at his wife and daughter. After he turned himself in for the 1992 killings, he blamed the crime on Sarge, one of several personalities he was convinced shared his body.

Scott Louis Panetti, a veteran of the U. S. Navy, was convicted of the murder of his mother-in-law and his father-in-law, the parents of his second wife, Sonja Alvarado. He then held his wife and daughter hostage for the night, but surrendered to police the next morning. Panetti was tried in a Texas state court for capital murder. Panetti sought to represent himself at which time the trial court ordered a competency hearing. Panetti was found to be suffering from a "fragmented personality, delusions, and hallucinations" for which he had been hospitalized over 12 times and for which he had been prescribed high doses of powerful psychiatric drugs for schizophrenia. Panetti's ex-wife testified at the competency hearing and described one of Panetti's psychotic episodes in 1986. During that episode, Panetti had "become convinced the devil had possessed their home and, in an effort to cleanse their surroundings, Panetti had buried a number of valuables next to the house and engaged in other rituals." Nonetheless, the trial judge found Panetti competent both to be tried and to waive his right to counsel. Trial judge did appoint a standby counsel to assist or even take over the defense if necessary. Panetti's defense at trial was that he was not guilty by reason of insanity. Standby counsel related that Panetti's behavior was "scary", "bizarre", and "trance-like." Based on Panetti's behavior both in private and before the jury, the standby attorney knew

---

March 2004.

that Panetti was not competent, and that his behavior made a farce and mockery of the judicial process.

Found guilty at trial, Panetti petitioned for a writ of habeas corpus in federal District Court, claiming mental illness. The Supreme Court had ruled in *Ford v. Wainwright* that execution of the mentally ill is barred by the Eighth Amendment's prohibition on cruel and unusual punishment. A psychiatric evaluation had found that Panetti believed that the State was "in league with the forces of evil" and was executing him in order to "prevent him from preaching the Gospel." However, the physicians also found that Panetti was aware of his crime, of the fact that he was to be executed, and of the State's stated reason for executing him. The District Court concluded that he was sufficiently sane to be executed.

On appeal, the U.S. Court of Appeals for the Fifth Circuit affirmed the lower court. The Fifth Circuit rejected Panetti's argument that an inmate cannot be executed if he lacks a rational understanding of the State's motivation for the execution. The Court of Appeals instead relied on Justice Lewis Powell's concurrence in Ford, holding that an inmate need only have an awareness of the State's reason for execution, not necessarily a rational understanding of it. Panetti raised the question as to whether the Eighth Amendment permits the execution of an inmate who has a factual awareness of the State's stated reason for his execution, but who lacks, due to mental illness, a rational understanding of the State's justification?[154]

Justice Anthony Kennedy wrote the Opinion of the Court for a 5-4 majority, and was joined by Justices Stevens, Ginsberg, Souter and Breyer. The Court held that the Fifth Circuit's analysis was too restrictive under *Ford v. Wainwright*, because it treated Panetti's mental condition as irrelevant as long as he had in some sense a factual awareness of the state's reasoning. The Court rejected the state's arguments that the Court did not have jurisdiction and that the state court was entitled to deference under

---

[154] Blumenthal, Ralph. "A Growing Plea for Mercy for the Mentally Ill on Death Row." *New York Times*, 23 November 2006; see also McCullugh, Jolie "Texas Death Row Inmate Scott Panetti to Get Further Competency Review" *Texas Tribune*, 11 July 2017; and Walker, Lauren, "Hours Before Controversial Execution of Scott Panetti" *Newsweek*, 3 December 2014.

the Antiterrorism and Effective Death Penalty Act of 1996 (AEDPA). In doing so, the Court held that a prisoner may bring a *habeas* petition claiming mental incompetency even if he had failed to make that claim in his first petition. State courts can be held to have unreasonably applied a legal principle even if the principle was addressed to somewhat different facts than those of the case at hand. The state court had unreasonably applied *Ford* by failing to give Panetti a fair hearing to fully present his psychiatric evidence. The Court also ruled that the Fifth Circuit "rests on a flawed interpretation of *Ford*," because it failed to consider that Panetti's delusions may have prevented him from understanding the meaning of his punishment even though he professed to be aware of the facts. The Court did not undertake its own analysis of what kind of rational understanding the Eighth Amendment requires a death row inmate to have, writing, "Although we reject the standard followed by the Court of Appeals, we do not attempt to set down a rule governing all competency determinations." The Court expressed the hope that expert psychiatric evidence would shed light on which delusions might distort an inmate's sense of reality so much as to render him incompetent to be executed.[155]

## Aileen Wuornos

Aileen Carol Wuornos Pralle, nèe Aileen Carol Pittman (1956–2002), was an American serial killer who murdered seven men in Florida between 1989 and 1990 by shooting them at point-blank range. In each case Wuornos claimed that her victims had either raped or attempted to rape her while she was working as a prostitute, and that all of the homicides were committed in self-defense. On January 14, 1992, Wuornos went to trial for the murder of one of her clients. Normally previous convictions are not admissible in criminal trials, but under Florida's Williams Rule the prosecution was allowed to introduce evidence related to her other crimes to show a pattern of illegal activity. On January 27, 1992, Wuornos was convicted of murder with help from testimony from her lesbian lover. At the trial psychiatrists testified that Wuornos was mentally unstable. She had previously been diagnosed with a borderline personality disorder and also an antisocial personality disorder. Four days

---

[155] *Panetti v Quarterman*, 551 US 930 (2007)

later, she was sentenced to death for six of the murders.

The case of Aileen Wuornos highlights some of the legal hurdles mentally ill capital defendants can face during their trial and appeals. Wuornos was never found legally insane, but her mental illness played a role in mitigation during her trial, and in her decision to waive her appeals.

Mental illness continued to be a dominant issue in the case after Wuornos was sentenced to death. Her mental health significantly deteriorated during her time on death row. Numerous attorneys appealed to the courts on her behalf, citing her bizarre and delusional behavior. In a letter to the Florida Supreme Court, Wuornos' appeals lawyer related, "In Court and at the jail, she exhibits bizarre behavior, laughing and crying at inappropriate times and obsessing on points having no importance to her cases." Wuornos herself wrote to the courts with apparently delusional claims of abuse by prison staff that included pressurizing chambers with "head shrinking" devices, harassment, and food cooked in dirt. She accused the staff of waging psychological and physical warfare against her. One of her attorneys wrote in a petition, "Petitioner's claims of prison abuse and mistreatment are either true or false. They are clearly believed to be true by Petitioner based upon her writings and behavior in Court on July 12, 2002. If true, Petitioner's claims must be resolved and corrected. If false, Petitioner's claims further support previous expert findings that she is delusional and mentally ill." In an October 8, 2002 interview with documentary filmmaker Nick Broomfield, Wuornos describes the alleged abuse that she claims she suffered in prison. Wuornos began to refuse to meet with mental health experts or her attorneys. She persistently filed petitions to waive her appeals and volunteered for execution in long rambling letters. A legal battle ensued over her competency to waive her appeals. Governor Jeb Bush ordered a 30-minute mental health assessment, conducted simultaneously by three experts. The three psychiatrists concluded Wuornos was competent to waive her appeals.[156]

Wuornos's execution took place on October 9, 2002. She declined her last meal and opted for a cup of coffee instead. Her last words

---

[156] "Mental Illness and the Death Penalty" https://capitalpunishmentincontext.org/node/77466

buttressed the contention that she was not sane: "Yes, I would just like to say I'm sailing with the rock, and I'll be back, like Independence Day, with Jesus. June 6, like the movie. Big mother ship and all, I'll be back, I'll be back."[157]

# Recent Cases

Cecil Clayton was executed on March 17, 2015, in Missouri, at age 74. Clayton suffered from dementia, had an IQ of 71, was missing a significant part of his brain due to an accident. His attorneys insisted he should be spared because he did not understand the nature and finality of the punishment. Clayton sustained a brain injury in a sawmill accident in 1972, requiring removal of about 20% of his frontal lobe, which is involved in impulse control, problem solving, and social behavior. After the accident, Clayton began experiencing violent impulses, schizophrenia, and extreme paranoia, which became so severe that he checked himself into a mental hospital out of fear he could not control his temper. In 1983, Dr. Douglas Stevens, a psychiatrist, examined Clayton and concluded, "There is presently no way that this man could be expected to function in the world of work. Were he pushed to do so he would become a danger both to himself and to others. He has had both suicidal and homicidal impulses, so far controlled, though under pressure they would be expected to exacerbate." In the past decade, six psychiatric evaluations have found that Clayton should be exempt from execution because he does not understand that he will be executed, or the reasons for his execution.[158]

John Ferguson was executed on August 5, 2013 in Florida although he had suffered from severe mental illness for more than four

---

[157] Howard, Peter. *Female Serial Killers: How and Why Women Become Monsters.* New York: Penguin, 2007, pp.142-43; also Silvio, Heather; McCloskey, Kathy; and Ramos-Grenier, Julia. "Theoretical Consideration of Female Sexual Predator Serial Killers in the United States". *Journal of Criminal Justice.* 34: 3, 251–259 (2006).

[158] Williams, T. "Lawyers Seek Reprieve for Killer Who Lost Part of His Brain Decades Earlier," *New York Times,* 7 March 2015; Rizzo, T. "Missouri Lawyers Say Man on Death Row is Mentally Incompetent Because of Sawmill Accident," *Kansas City Star*, 8 March 2015. See also https://deathpenaltyinfo.org/mental-illness-and-death-penalty#executions

decades. As early as 1965, Ferguson was found to experience visual hallucinations. At various mental institutions he was diagnosed as paranoid schizophrenic, delusional, and aggressive. In 1975, a psychiatrist described Ferguson as "dangerous and cannot be released under any circumstances." Nevertheless, he was released less than a year later. Ferguson hallucinates that he is the "Prince of God" and by being executed he can save the world.[159] Frank Spisak, a self-proclaimed Nazi who killed three people at Cleveland State University nearly 30 years ago in a racism-fueled rampage, was executed by injection Thursday morning. Spisak expressed no remorse for his crimes when given a chance to say his final words. Instead, he read a handwritten note -- in German -- with verses one through seven of Chapter 21 in the Bible's Book of Revelations. Spisak, who wore a Hitler-style moustache and saluted the Nazi leader during his 1983 trial, struggled at times to read the note clearly, complaining that the words were blurry. He spent more than 27 years on death row. Over the course of several months in 1982, Spisak, driven by his Nazi beliefs, killed three people. Spisak would go on "hunting parties" and targeted victims because they were black. After his execution, his lawyers said "The media will focus on the 'Nazi' propaganda of the prosecution [but] the truth is [Spisak] was seriously mentally ill and committed the crimes because of this mental illness, not because of hate.[160]

Garry Allen was executed in Oklahoma on November 6, 2012. His execution has been stayed repeatedly due to questions about his mental competence. He had been diagnosed with schizophrenia as well as dementia caused by seizures, drug abuse, and a gunshot wound to his head sustained during his arrest. In 2008, the Oklahoma Pardon and Parole Board recommended that his death sentence be commuted by a 4-1 vote. Governor Mary Fallin granted a stay in order to consider the Board's recommendation, but denied clemency. Allen murdered his wife 26 years ago, after she had left him and taken their two children.[161]

---

[159] "State Shouldn't Execute Severely Mentally Ill Killer," *Tampa Bay Times,* 27 November 2012.

[160] Guillen, Joe. "Frank Spisak Executed for 1982 Slayings of Three People at Cleveland State University", *Cleveland Plain Dealer*, 17 February 2011

[161] Petersen, R. "Oklahoma Death Row Inmate Executed" *McAlester News-*

Jared Lee Loughner of Tucson was charged for the murder of a federal judge and a Congressional staff member, as well as for causing the deaths of four other participants Judge Roll and Gabriel M. Zimmerman, and for Dorothy J. Morris, Phyllis C. Schneck, Dorwan C. Stoddard. He also caused injuries to others during his alleged attempt to assassinate U.S. Representative Gabrielle D. Giffords. Loughner, 22, attempted to assassinate Rep. Giffords and attempted to murder two federal employees who worked for Giffords, District Director Ronald S. Barber and Community Outreach Coordinator Pamela K. Simon.[162]

From the outset the government saw this as a potential death-penalty case, so it pursued a deliberate and thorough examination. That process is ongoing, and we will continue to work diligently to see that justice is done." He was examined by several psychiatrists and psychologists and found to be a paranoid schizophrenic and unlikely to be cured. He was so belligerent that the government sought to administer strong anti-psychotic drugs. He became violent, spitting on and cursing his lawyer.[163] Eventually Loughner was found incompetent to stand trial, especially in a death penalty case. He pled guilty to killing six people and wounding an additional thirteen persons. By plea agreement he will spend the rest of his life in prison and will not appeal his sentence.[164]

---

*Capital*, 7 November 2012.

[162] Original indictment in the U.S. Dist. Ct. (Ariz.) Jan. 19, 2011.

[163] Franklin, K. "Loughner Case Shines Spotlight on Forced Meds Practices," *Forensic Psychology, Criminology, and Psychology-law*, 10 July 2011; Goldstein, J. and Lacey, M. "To Defend the Accused in a Tucson Rampage, First a Battle to Get Inside a Mind," *New York Times*, 12 February 2011.

[164] *New York Daily News*, 7 August 2012; J. Cloherty, J., Thomas P., and Balderick T., "Jared Lee Loughner Mentally Incompetent to Stand Trial in Deadly Arizona Shootings," ABC News, 25 2011; Emshwiller, J and Audi, T, "Loughner's Mental Competence is Doubted," *Wall Street Journal*, 17 May 2011.

# Intelligence and Culpability

The Founding Fathers, Framers of the U.S. Constitution, and Sages who created the common law tradition have long held that it was "cruel to execute idiots. Legal giants, such as Blackstone, Coke, and Story, described the execution of these disabled people as "savage and inhuman," leading to a "miserable spectacle," which was "of extreme inhumanity and cruelty." The courts must who qualifies as an "idiot" for purposes of capital punishment.

Mental retardation is all pervasive in the life of the impaired individual's life. At its most intensive level, it can be completely debilitating. Professional diagnosis of mental retardation is undertaken in stages. First, the individual is administered a standard IQ test which results in assignment of a number. Second, professionals measure the person's adaptive skills, with an eye to identifying various strengths and weaknesses. Third, professionals attempt to determine at what age the condition was first observed.

Three criteria are necessary for a diagnosis of mental retardation: First, there must be an IQ score of 70 to 75 or lower. Second, there must be consequential limitations in at least several crucial areas of adaptive skills, which include communication, self-care, home living, social skills, community use, self-direction, health and safety, functional academics, leisure, and work. Third, the disability must have become obvious before the person arrived at the age of eighteen.

Once a diagnosis of mental retardation has been made, the person is classified according to the severity, which depends heavily upon the IQ score. Mild retardation includes those with an IQ score of 50-55 to 70-75. The mildly retarded have an estimated mental age equivalent to that of an eight- to twelve-year-old normal functioning child. Their language ability is fluent by adolescence, their reading and arithmetic skills remain between first and sixth grade levels, and they are generally able to live and work independently. About 89% of mentally retarded people are classified as mildly retarded.[165]

Moderate retardation includes those with an IQ score of 35-40 to 50-55. Moderately retarded individuals possess the mental age of a six- to eight-year-old child. Their language ability is functional by adolescence, although practical reading and arithmetic abilities are not attained, and they require some supervision in everyday living. Persons achieving levels below this are rarely encountered in the criminal justice system.[166]

There has been much published literature and there have been many debates about the role that insanity plays in a person's actions, but there has been only limited discussion regarding the significance of mental retardation upon the culpability of a criminal defendant. Insanity may be only a temporary mental illness, but mental retardation is ordinarily a permanent mental disability. For the law especially the essential difference between mental illness and mental retardation is that mentally ill people encounter disturbances in their thought processes and emotions; mentally retarded people have limited abilities to learn. Certainly many people with average to high intelligence can become mentally ill. However, most mentally retarded people are not, and will not become, mentally ill. This distinction is significant. Mental retardation affects the very tool necessary to obtain knowledge and thus the ability to learn. With a limited learning ability, the mentally retarded defendant has difficulty synthesizing all of the information presented to him in his lifetime. A mentally retarded person can learn and comprehend information. It is more difficult,

[165] Freedman, Allison. "Mental Retardation and the Death Penalty: The Need for an International Standard Defining Mental Retardation," 12 N W. J. Int'l Hum. Rts. 1 (2014); Entzeroth, Lyn. "Constitutional Prohibition on the Execution of the Mentally Retarded Criminal Defendant," Tulsa L. Rev. 38: 299 (2013).
[166] See Billotte, Jamie M. "Is It Justified - The Death Penalty and Mental Retardation", Notre Dame J. L. Ethics & Pub. Pol'y 8: 333 (1994).

however, than if he was not retarded. This learning process may take years longer for a retarded person than a non-retarded person.[167]

## A Modern Case

Ricky Ray Rector (1950--1992), was executed on January 24, 1992 for the 1981 murder of a police officer Robert Martin in Conway, Arkansas. In 1981, Ricky Ray Rector decided to rob a convenience store. After murdering a man in a restaurant, Ricky Ray Rector duped a police officer into believing that he would surrender for his crime. Instead he shot the officer in the back before turning the gun on himself in an attempted suicide. He survived a gunshot wound to the head, but was left intellectually impaired. Later, his IQ would be measured at around 70 which is also the benchmark for determining mental retardation. Rector was black, adding to racial questions relating to the death penalty.[168]

Former Arkansas governor William Jefferson Clinton came back to Arkansas in order to preside over Rector's execution during his 1992 presidential race. Many consider it a turning point in that race, hardening Clinton's reportedly soft public image.[169]

Rector's mental insufficiency was clearly shown by what he told officers on the day of his execution. Having chosen a meal that consisted of steak, fried chicken, pecan pie, and cherry Kool-Aid, Rector instructed the correction officers to refrain from disposing of the pecan pie until after his execution. He indicated that he was saving his pecan pie for later.

Rector was executed by lethal injection on January 24, 1992. It took medical staff, with Rector's help, more than fifty minutes to find a suitable vein in Rector's arm. The curtain remained closed between Rector and the witnesses, but some reported they could hear Rector moaning. The team of two medical people, which had grown to five, worked on both sides of his body to find a vein. The state later attributed the difficulty in finding a suitable vein to Rector's heavy weight and

---

[167] Bordenave, F. and Kelly, D. "Death Penalty and Mentally Ill Defendants," *Journal of the American Academy of Psychiatry and the Law*, (2010).

[168] *Rector v Clark*, 923 F.2d 570 (1991)

[169] Applebome, Peter "Death Penalty; Arkansas Execution Raises Questions on Governor's Politics", *New York Times*, 25 January 1992.

to his use of an anti-psychotic medication.[170]

## *Penry v. Lynaugh*

On October 25, 1979, Pamela Carpenter was brutally raped, beaten, and stabbed in her home in Livingston, Texas. She died a few hours later in the course of emergency treatment. But before she died, she described her assailant which deputy sheriffs to suspect Penry, who had recently been released on parole after conviction on another rape charge. Penry subsequently gave two statements confessing to the crime, and was charged with capital murder.

At a competency hearing held before trial, a clinical psychologist, Dr. Jerome Brown, testified that Penry was mentally retarded. As a child, Penry was diagnosed as having organic brain damage, which was probably caused by trauma to the brain at birth. Penry was tested over the years as having an IQ between 50 and 63, which indicates mild to moderate retardation. Dr. Brown's own testing indicated that Penry had an IQ of 54. Dr. Brown stated that Penry had the mental age of a 6 1/2-year-old child. Penry's social maturity, or ability to function in the world, was that of a 9- or 10-year-old.

Despite the diagnosis the state charged Penry with capital murder. At the guilt-innocence phase of the trial, petitioner raised an insanity defense and presented psychiatric testimony that he suffered from a combination of organic brain damage and moderate retardation which resulted in poor impulse control and an inability to learn from experience. He had been abused as a child. The State introduced testimony that petitioner was legally sane, but had an antisocial personality. The jury rejected petitioner's insanity defense and found him guilty of capital murder.

At the penalty phase of the trial, the sentencing jury was instructed to consider all the evidence introduced at trial in answering the following "special issues": (1) whether petitioner's conduct was committed deliberately and with the reasonable expectation that death would result; (2) whether there was a probability that he would be a continuing threat to

---

[170] http://murderpedia.org/male.R/r1/rector-ricky-ray.htm

society; and (3) whether the killing was unreasonable in response to any provocation by the victim. The trial court rejected petitioner's request for jury instructions defining mercy based upon the existence of mitigating circumstances. The jury answered "yes" to each special issue, and, as required by Texas law, the court therefore sentenced petitioner to death.

The Texas Court of Criminal Appeals affirmed, rejecting petitioner's contentions that his death sentence violated the Eighth Amendment first, because the jury was not adequately instructed to consider all of his mitigating evidence and because the special issues' terms were not defined in such a way that the jury could consider and give effect to that evidence in answering them; and, second, because it is cruel and unusual punishment to execute a mentally retarded person with petitioner's mental ability.

After the Texas court denied *certiorari* on direct review, the Federal District Court and the Court of Appeals upheld petitioner's death sentence in *habeas corpus* proceedings. Although it denied him relief, the Court of Appeals nevertheless found considerable merit in petitioner's claim that his mitigating evidence of mental retardation and childhood abuse could not be given effect by the jury, under the instructions given, in answering the special issues.[171]

The U. S. Supreme Court ruled that the execution of the mentally retarded does not violate the Eighth Amendment's ban on cruel and unusual punishments. Justice O'Conner wrote the Opinion of the Court. The Court ruled that Texas juries must, upon request, be given instructions that allow them to give effect to that mitigating evidence in determining whether to impose the death penalty. [172] Justice O'Conner wrote,

> The Eighth Amendment's categorical prohibition upon the infliction of cruel and unusual punishment applies to practices condemned by the common law at the time the

---

[171] Bing, Jonathan L. "Protecting the Mentally Retarded from Capital Punishment: State Efforts Since Penry and Recommendations for the Future". N.Y.U. Review of Law & Social Change. 22:1 at 59–151 (1996); Hagenah, Patricia (1990). "Imposing the Death Sentence on Mentally Retarded Defendants: The Case of Penry v. Lynaugh". *UMKC Law Review.* 59: 1 at 135–153 (1990).

[172] *Penry v. Lynaugh*, 492 U.S. 302 (1989)

Bill of Rights was adopted, as well as to punishments which offend our society's evolving standards of decency as expressed in objective evidence of legislative enactments and the conduct of sentencing juries. Since the common law prohibited the punishment of "idiots" - which term was generally used to describe persons totally lacking in reason, understanding, or the ability to distinguish between good and evil - it may indeed be "cruel and unusual punishment" to execute persons who are profoundly or severely retarded and wholly lacking in the capacity to appreciate the wrongfulness of their actions. Such persons, however, are not likely to be convicted or face the prospect of punishment today, since the modern insanity defense generally includes "mental defect" as part of the legal definition of insanity . . . . [The law] prohibits the execution of persons who are unaware of their punishment and why they must suffer it. Moreover, petitioner is not such a person, since the jury (1) found him competent to stand trial and therefore to have a rational as well as factual understanding of the proceedings; and (2) rejected his insanity defense, thereby reflecting the conclusion that he knew his conduct was wrong and was capable of conforming it to the requirements of law. Nor is there sufficient objective evidence today of a national consensus against executing mentally retarded capital murderers, since petitioner has cited only one state statute that explicitly bans that practice and has offered no evidence of the general behavior of juries in this regard. Opinion surveys indicating strong public opposition to such executions do not establish a societal consensus, absent some legislative reflection of the sentiment expressed therein.[173]

Thus the same day the Court decided *Stanford*, it held that the Eighth Amendment did not mandate a categorical exemption from the death penalty for the mentally retarded. In reaching this conclusion it stressed that only two States had enacted laws banning the imposition of the death penalty on a mentally retarded person convicted of a capital

---

[173] *Id* at 330-335.

offense. According to the Court, "the two state statutes prohibiting execution of the mentally retarded, even when added to the fourteen States that have rejected capital punishment completely, [did] not provide sufficient evidence at present of a national consensus."[174]

In 2002, the Supreme Court considered whether the special characteristics of individuals with mental retardation requires that they be categorically exempted from the death penalty as a matter of federal constitutional law. In holding that the execution of a mentally retarded persons is a constitutionally forbidden Cruel and Unusual Punishment, the Court asserted that "because of their disabilities in areas of reasoning, judgment, and control of their impulses, they do not act with a level of moral culpability that characterizes the more serious adult criminal conduct." The standard put forth in *Atkins* was not lack of legal responsibility—for individuals with mental retardation often know the difference between right and wrong—but of diminished criminal culpability. Because of their mental impairments, they "have a diminished capacity to understand and process information, to abstract from mistakes and learn from experience, to engage in logical reasoning, to control impulses, and to understand the reactions of others.... Their deficiencies do not warrant an exemption from criminal sanctions, but they do diminish their criminal culpability."[175]

Victim's rights advocates protested a further narrowing of the number of individuals who were eligible for the death penalty. A number of attorneys general in states that allowed the execution of juvenile defendants and the Texas-based Justice for All organization submitted amicus briefs in the Roper case requesting that the Supreme Court uphold Stanford. In addition, they argued that the Court should not group juveniles together as a class of defendants, but instead "acknowledge that they are all different with respect to their experience, maturity, intelligence and moral culpability."

## *Atkins v. Virginia*

Daryl Renard Atkins, was convicted of abduction, armed robbery,

---

[174] *Penry v. Lynaugh*, 492 U.S. 302 (1989)
[175] *Atkins v. Virginia* (2002)

and capital murder, and sentenced to death. At approximately midnight on August 16, 1996, Atkins and William Jones, armed with a semiautomatic handgun, abducted Eric Nesbitt, robbed him of the money and drove him to an automated teller machine in his pickup truck where cameras recorded their withdrawal of additional cash. They then took him to an isolated location where he was shot eight times and killed.

Jones and Atkins both testified in the guilt phase of Atkins' trial. Each confirmed most of the details in the other's account of the incident, with the important exception that each stated that the other had actually shot and killed Nesbitt.

The jury found Jones' testimony both more coherent and credible than that of Atkins and was sufficient to establish Atkins' guilt. At the penalty phase of the trial, the State introduced victim impact evidence that helped to prove two aggravating circumstances: future dangerousness and "vileness of the offense." To prove future dangerousness, the State relied on Atkins' prior felony convictions as well as the testimony of four victims of earlier robberies and assaults. To prove the second factor, the prosecution relied upon the trial record, including pictures of the deceased's body and the autopsy report. For its part the defense relied on only one witness, Dr. Evan Nelson, a forensic psychologist who had evaluated Atkins before trial and concluded that he was "mildly mentally retarded." Dr. Nelson based his conclusion on interviews with people who knew Atkins, a review of school and court records, and the administration of a standard intelligence test which indicated that Atkins had a full scale IQ of 59.5.

Atkins was convicted of capital murder and related crimes by a Virginia jury and sentenced to death.[176] Affirming, the Virginia Supreme Court relied on *Penry*[177] in rejecting Atkins' contention that he could not be sentenced to death because he is mentally retarded.

Since *Penry* a significant number of States have concluded that death is not a suitable punishment for mentally retarded criminals. It is not only the number of states that have changed their laws that is significant,

---

[176] 260 Va. 375, 534 S. E. 2d 312
[177] *Penry v. Lynaugh*, 492 U.S. 302

but the consistency of the direction of change. Given the fact that anti-crime legislation is far more popular than legislation protecting criminals, the large number of states prohibiting the execution of mentally retarded persons provides powerful evidence that today society views mentally retarded offenders as categorically less culpable than the average criminal. Conversely, there is a complete absence of legislation reinstating such executions. In the state legislatures addressing the issue, their legislators have voted overwhelmingly in favor of the prohibition. Even in such states that still allow the execution of mentally retarded offenders, the practice is uncommon.

Accordingly, the Supreme Court found no reason to disagree with the legislative consensus. It then gave its reasons for supporting the change: Clinical definitions of mental retardation require not only sub average intellectual functioning, but also significant limitations in adaptive skills. Mentally retarded persons frequently know the difference between right and wrong and are competent to stand trial, but, by definition, they have diminished capacities to understand and process information, to communicate, to abstract from mistakes and learn from experience, to engage in logical reasoning, to control impulses, and to understand others' reactions. Their deficiencies do not warrant an exemption from criminal sanctions, but diminish their personal culpability. In light of these deficiencies, the Court's death penalty jurisprudence provides two reasons to agree with the legislative consensus.

The Court held that there is a serious question whether either justification underpinning the death penalty–retribution and deterrence of capital crimes–applies to mentally retarded offenders. As to retribution, the severity of the appropriate punishment necessarily depends on the offender's culpability. If the culpability of the average murderer is insufficient to justify imposition of death, the lesser culpability of the mentally retarded offender surely does not merit that form of retribution. As to deterrence, the same cognitive and behavioral impairments that make mentally retarded defendants less morally culpable also make it less likely that they can process the information of the possibility of execution as a penalty and, as a result, control their conduct based upon that information. Nor will exempting the mentally retarded from execution lessen the death penalty's deterrent effect with respect to offenders who are not mentally retarded. Second, mentally retarded defendants in the aggregate face a special risk of wrongful execution because of the possibility that they will unwittingly confess to crimes they did not commit, their lesser ability to give their counsel meaningful assistance, and the facts that they are typically poor witnesses and that their demeanor may create an unwarranted impression of lack of remorse for their crimes.[178]

## *Hall v. Florida*

In 1978, Freddie Lee Hall and an accomplice kidnapped, beat, raped, and murdered a woman in Florida. Hall and his accomplice then drove to a convenience store they planned to rob, and killed a sheriff's deputy who attempted to apprehend them in the process. Hall was convicted in 1978 and received the death penalty for both murders, but his sentence for the second murder was later reduced. The Florida legislature had enacted a statute [179] in 2001, prohibiting death sentences for individuals with intellectual disabilities. Hall presented evidence of intellectual disability including school records, multiple attorneys' records and briefs, medical and clinical opinions, and siblings' testimony at a re-sentencing hearing. The state of Florida sentenced Freddie Lee Hall to death on September 9, 1982 for murdering Karol Hurst. Even after hearing such evidence, the jury and judge again sentenced Hall to death in 1991.

Hall filed a motion in 2004 in the Supreme Court of Florida claiming that he had an intellectual disability and could not be executed. At this new hearing, Hall again presented evidence of his intellectual disability, this time including several IQ scores. Of the nine IQ evaluations he offered, with scores ranging from 60 to 80, the sentencing court excluded the two scores below 70 for evidentiary reasons. This left only scores between 71 and 80. Because Florida law required Hall to show an IQ test score of 70 or below before he would be allowed to present additional evidence of his intellectual disability, the

---

[178] *Atkins v. Virginia*, 536 U.S. 304 (2002)
[179] § 921.137

Florida Supreme Court rejected Hall's appeal.[180]

In 2013, Hall appealed to the U.S. Supreme Court on a constitutional basis. Hall argued that Flora was derelict in three ways in its duty to properly evaluate his abilities or lack thereof. First, instead of weighing the three prongs of the Atkins analysis simultaneously, the Florida courts used this prong as a barrier to the other two. Thus, if an individual's IQ test score is above 70, that person does not have an intellectual disability and is barred from presenting other evidence that would show his intellectual abilities are limited. The Florida statute used the IQ score as "final and conclusive evidence" of intellectual disability, even though experts might consider other evidence concurrently.

Second, the Court noted that the professionals who designed, administered, and interpreted IQ tests concluded that each individual IQ test has a standard error of measurement. This statistical fact reflects that an individual's intellectual functioning cannot be reduced to a single numerical score, and thus an individual's score is best understood as a range on either side of that recorded score. According the American Psychological Association (APA) employs a margin for error of +/- 5 points.

The actions of other states demonstrate that Florida's strict interpretation is not the interpretation employed by the majority of states. The court noted that in 41 States an individual in Hall's IQ score of 71 would not be considered eligible for the death penalty.[181]

The U.S. Supreme Court ruled that Florida's courts were interpreting its own law unconstitutionally. Florida's courts used the IQ score as a barrier to reviewing further evidence of intellectual capacity, did not acknowledge that the score could be imprecise or allow for a range instead of a specific number score, and did not comport with the practices

---

[180] *Hall v. State*, 614 So. 2d 473, 479 (Fla. 1993)
[181] *Hall v. Florida*, 134 S. Ct. 1986 (2014)

of the majority of other states.[182]

---

[182] Bazelon, Emily, "The Death Penalty Just Got a Tiny Bit Saner: Today's Supreme Court Decision Makes It Harder for States to Execute the Mentally Disabled." *Slate,* 27 May 2014; See also Cooke, Brian K., Delalot, Dominque and Werner, Tonia L. "Hall v. Florida: Capital Punishment, IQ, and Persons With Intellectual Disabilities" *Journal of the American Academy of Psychiatry and the Law Online*, 43: 2 at 230-234 (June 2015).

# Who Imposes the Death Penalty?

Who indeed should impose the death penalty in the name of We the People? Someone or some group is ultimately responsible for determining that a defendant is the correct recipient of society's ultimate penalty. In his classic defense of Leopold and Loeb, brilliant defense attorney Clarence Darrow asked for trial by judge rather than jury. Knowing his clients not only to be absolutely guilty, but almost certainly to be found fully culpable in a trial. Darrow thought that he could more effectively argue against the death penalty before one man rather than before twelve worthy citizens. Responsibility would rest wholly upon one man rather than being divided among many. In the earlier days of our Republic it seemed to matter little who imposed, or chose to not impose, the death sentence. In more recent times, since the reintroduction of the possibility of a death sentence it has become enormously important who imposes capital punishment.

## *Ring v. Arizona*

On November 28, 1994, two robbers approached an armored car parked in front of Arrowhead Mall in Glendale, Arizona. They shot the driver, John Magoch, in the head as he exited the van to smoke, and died almost instantly. One of the robbers then drove the van to a church in nearby Sun City, where they made off with $562,000 in cash and $271,000 in personal checks. An informant tipped the police off to Timothy Ring and two of his friends, who had recently made expensive purchases such as a new truck. Police eventually discovered that Ring was the ringleader of the operation. Ring was later charged with capital felony murder under Arizona law.

The jury eventually convicted Ring of felony murder. But Ring could not be sentenced to death without further findings, and Arizona law provided that the judge alone would make these findings. After a sentencing hearing, at which Ring's accomplices testified, the judge found that two aggravating factors applied: that Ring had committed the murder in expectation of pecuniary gain and that he had committed the murder in an especially heinous, cruel, or depraved manner. Although he found that Ring had a "minimal" criminal record, the judge concluded that this did not outweigh the aggravating factors, and sentenced Ring to death.

In a 7-2 decision in the case of *Ring v. Arizona*, the U.S. Supreme Court held that a defendant has the right to have a jury, rather than a judge, decide on the existence of an aggravating factor that makes the defendant eligible for the death penalty. The Court based its judgment on the broader constitutional principle that the Sixth Amendment right to trial by jury encompasses the right to a jury finding of all facts that are necessary to put a defendant to death. In its decision, the Court held that Arizona's sentencing statute, under which the judge determined the presence or absence of aggravating factors necessary to make a defendant eligible for the death penalty violated this Sixth Amendment guarantee.[183]

At Timothy Ring's trial for murder, the jury deadlocked on premeditated murder, but found Ring guilty of felony murder occurring in the course of armed robbery. Under Arizona law, Ring could not be sentenced to death, unless further findings were made by a judge conducting a separate sentencing hearing and only if the judge finds at least one aggravating circumstance and no mitigating circumstances sufficiently substantial to call for leniency. Because the jury had convicted Ring of felony murder, not premeditated murder, Ring would be eligible for the death penalty only if he was the victim's actual killer. Citing accomplice testimony at the sentencing hearing, the judge found that Ring was the killer. The judge then found two aggravating factors, one of them being that the offense was committed for pecuniary gain, as well as one mitigating factor, Ring's minimal criminal record, and ruled that the latter did not call for leniency.

---

[183] Associated Press, June 24, 2002

In appealing to the U.S. Supreme Court Ring argued that Arizona's capital sentencing scheme violated the Sixth Amendment's jury trial guarantee by entrusting to a judge the finding of facts sufficient to impose the death penalty.

Justice Ruth Bader Ginsburg wrote the opinion of the court. Because Arizona's enumerated aggravating factors operates as "the functional equivalent of an element of a greater offense," the Sixth Amendment requires that they be found by a jury. Under *Apprendi v. New Jersey* [184] the Sixth Amendment does not permit a defendant to be "exposed...to a penalty exceeding the maximum he would receive if punished according to the facts reflected in the jury verdict alone," the Court overruled *Walton v. Arizona,* 497 U.S. 639, insofar it allows a sentencing judge, sitting without a jury, to find an aggravating circumstance necessary for imposition of the death penalty. "The right to trial by jury guaranteed by the Sixth Amendment would be senselessly diminished if it encompassed the fact-finding necessary to increase a defendant's sentence by two years, but not the fact finding necessary to put him to death," wrote Justice Ginsburg.

The high court's 7-2 decision in *Ring* ended the practice of having a judge, rather than a jury, decide whether there are "aggravating factors" in a case that can justify a death penalty. The court ruled that determining such factors is essentially a finding of fact, a power traditionally left to juries. However, Ring vs. Arizona was soon interpreted in 3 differing ways by the 9th, 6th and 11th circuit courts of appeal. The U.S. Supreme Court agreed to clarify the impact of its 2002 *Ring v. Arizona* ruling that held that jurors, rather than a judge, must be allowed to determine whether a defendant is eligible for a death sentence. The Justices will decide whether the U.S. Court of Appeals for the 9th Circuit was correct when it overturned Warren Summerlin's death sentence, holding that Ring should apply retroactively to inmates who had exhausted their direct appeal. While the Supreme Court's Ring ruling invalidated the death sentencing laws of Arizona, Montana, Idaho, Nebraska and Colorado, it did not make clear if its ruling should apply retroactively to everyone on those states'

---

[184] *Apprendi v. New Jersey,* 530 U.S. 466

death rows. Since the decision, courts have issued differing interpretations on the retro-activity question.

Justice Sandra Day O'Connor argued that the Court's decision would have serious consequences, opening up a flood of litigation from death-row inmates and creating uncertainty in the laws of nine other states that employed either total or partial judicial fact-finding in death sentences.[185]

## Schriro v. Summerlin

The United States Supreme Court has granted certiorari on two questions in the case of Schriro v. Summerlin.[186] The two questions are: Did the Ninth Circuit err by holding that the new rule announced in Ring is substantive, rather than procedural, and therefore exempt from the retro-activity analysis of Teague? [187] Did the Ninth Circuit err by holding that the new rule announced in Ring applies retroactively to cases on collateral review under Teague's exception for watershed rules of criminal procedure that alter bedrock procedural principles and seriously enhance the accuracy of the proceedings?

In April 1981, Finance America employee Brenna Bailey disappeared while on a house call to discuss an outstanding debt with respondent Warren Summerlin's wife. That evening, an anonymous woman, later identified as Summerlin's mother-in-law, called the police and accused respondent of murdering Bailey. Bailey's partially nude body, her skull crushed, was found the next morning in the trunk of her car, wrapped in a bedspread from respondent's home. Police arrested Summerlin. Adding to his culpability, police later overheard Summerlin make incriminating remarks to his wife. Summerlin was convicted of first-degree murder and sexual assault. Arizona's capital sentencing provisions in effect at the time authorized the death penalty if one of several enumerated aggravating factors was present as was the case here.

In a 5-4 decision on June 24, 2004, the Supreme Court determined that its 2002 decision in Ring v. Arizona was not retroactive, thereby

---

[185] Associated Press, December 1, 2003
[186] Schriro v. Summerlin, No. 03-526 (formerly Summerlin v. Stewart)
[187] Teague v. Lane, 489 U.S. 288 (1989)

denying new sentencing hearings for dozens of death row inmates in Arizona, Idaho, Montana and Nebraska whose sentences were originally handed down by judges, but whose cases are older and not in the first stages of their appeals. In *Ring*, the Court decided that sentencing laws must protect the right to a jury determination of eligibility for the death penalty. With their decision in *Summerlin*,[188] the Justices decided that their original 7-2 decision in *Ring* was a procedural rule and thus was not retroactive. Justice A. Scalia wrote the opinion of the Court. He wrote, "The right to jury trial is fundamental to our system of criminal procedure, and States are bound to enforce the Sixth Amendment's guarantees as we interpret them. But it does not follow that, when a criminal defendant has had a full trial and one round of appeals in which the State faithfully applied the Constitution as we understood it at the time, he may nevertheless continue to litigate his claims indefinitely in hopes that we will one day have a change of heart. Ring announced a new procedural rule that does not apply retroactively to cases already final on direct review. "Thus the contrary judgment of the Ninth Circuit was reversed, and the case is remanded for further proceedings consistent with this opinion. Dissenting in *Summerlin* were Justices Stevens, Souter, Ginsburg and Breyer. Discussing the differences between the death row inmates granted new sentencing hearings and the death row inmates denied new sentencing hearings because they are in a later stage of appeals, Justice Breyer stated: "Certainly the ordinary citizen will not understand the difference. That citizen will simply witness two individuals, both sentenced through the use of unconstitutional procedures, one individual going to his death, the other saved, all through an accident of timing. How can the Court square this spectacle with what it has called the 'vital importance to the defendant and to the community that any decision to impose the death sentence be, and appear to be, based on reason'?"

## *Hurst v. Florida*

In an 8-1 decision in *Hurst v. Florida* released on January 12, 2016, the U.S. Supreme Court found Florida's capital sentencing scheme in violation of the 6th Amendment, which guarantees the right to trial by jury."

---

[188] *Schriro v. Summerlin*, No. 03-526 (2004).

The Sixth Amendment requires a jury, not a judge, to find each fact necessary to impose a sentence of death."

A Florida jury convicted Timothy Hurst of first-degree murder for killing a co-worker and recommended the death penalty. The court sentenced Hurst to death, but he was granted a new sentencing hearing on appeal. At the re-sentencing hearing, the jury again recommended death, and the judge again found the facts necessary to sentence Hurst to death. The Florida Supreme Court affirmed, rejecting Hurst's argument that his sentence violated the Sixth Amendment.[189]

Justice Sonia Sotomayor wrote in the opinion of the Court. The jury and judge in Hurst's case followed Florida's statutory sentencing procedure, which requires only an "advisory sentence" from a jury. Florida does not require the jury to specify the factual basis of its sentencing recommendation. The sentencing judge must give "great weight" to the jury's recommendation, but only the judge ever provides written reasons why a case is eligible for a death sentence. The Court based its decision largely on *Ring v. Arizona*, a 2002 decision in which it struck down Arizona's sentencing scheme because a judge, rather than a jury, determined the facts necessary to impose a death sentence. While Florida's procedure adds the advisory recommendation that Arizona's lacked, the Court found the distinction, "immaterial." Justice Sotomayor wrote, "In arguing that the jury's recommendation necessarily included an aggravating circumstance finding, Florida fails to appreciate the judge's central and singular role under Florida law, which makes the court's findings necessary to impose death and makes the jury's function advisory only. The State cannot now treat the jury's advisory recommendation as the necessary factual finding required by Ring." Her opinion continued, "As with Timothy Ring, the maximum punishment Timothy Hurst could have received without any judge-made findings was life in prison without parole. As with Ring, a judge increased Hurst's authorized punishment based on her own fact finding. In light of Ring, we hold that Hurst's sentence violates the Sixth Amendment."

---

[189] Barnes, R. "Supreme Court finds Florida's capital punishment process unconstitutional," *Washington Post*, January 12, 2016

Justice Breyer concurred with the Court's decision, but would find that the Eighth Amendment requires that a jury determine the actual sentence, not just the facts that make a person eligible for death. He wrote, "I concur in the judgment here based on my view that "the Eighth Amendment requires that a jury, not a judge, make the decision to sentence a defendant to death."

Justice Alito dissented, citing past decisions upholding Florida's death penalty statute. Justice Alito wrote, "this Court 'repeatedly has reviewed and upheld Florida's capital sentencing statute over the past quarter of a century. . . . And as the Court also concedes, our precedents hold that "'the Sixth Amendment does not require that the specific findings authorizing the imposition of the sentence of death be made by the jury.' . . . The Court now reverses course, striking down Florida's capital sentencing system, overruling our decisions in *Hildwin* and *Spaziano*, and holding that the Sixth Amendment does require that the specific findings authorizing a sentence of death be made by a jury. I disagree."[190]

In March 2016, the Florida legislature directly addressed *Hurst* by requiring that jurors unanimously find any aggravating circumstances that the prosecution seeks to prove to make the defendant eligible for the death penalty. It also modified Florida's sentencing practice by requiring that at least ten jurors recommend death before the judge may impose a death sentence.

## Victim Impact Statements

A victim impact statement is a written or oral statement made as part of the judicial legal process, which allows crime victims the opportunity to speak during the sentencing of the convicted person or at subsequent parole hearings. A victim impact statement includes a description of the physical and emotional damage caused by the crime, the financial costs incurred by the victim, and the medical treatments required for him or his family.[191]

In May of 1984, John Booth and Willie Reid entered the home of

---

[190] *Hurst v Florida,* No. 14-7505 (2016)
[191] From the National Center for the Victims of Crimes.

Irvin and Rose Bronstein for the purpose of stealing money to buy heroin. Booth, who lived only three houses away in the same neighborhood, was aware that the Bronsteins could identify him, so he and Reid stabbed the elderly couple to death. He was found guilty of two counts of first-degree murder, two counts of robbery, and conspiracy to commit robbery. After the trial, Booth opted to let the jury determine his sentence instead of the judge.

Before the sentencing phase began, the State Division of Parole and Probation presented a report that was required by state statute. Information required in the report included a victim impact statement (VIS) that described the effect of the crime on the victims and the victims' family. The VIS was either read to the jury, or the family members offered their views orally by appearing in court. In this case, the VIS was based on a statement by the victims' son, daughter, son-in-law, and granddaughter. The Bronstein family told about the warmness of Irvin and Rose and about all the problems that members of the family suffered due to their loss. In their VIS, the family also offered opinions and characterizations of the crimes and their opinions about the persons who committed the crime. In one part of the VIS, the Bronsteins' daughter said "I don't feel that the people who did this could ever be rehabilitated and I don't want them to be able to do this again."

On appeal, the Maryland Court of Appeals affirmed the lower court's decision, finding that the VIS "serves an important interest by informing the sentence of the full measure of harm caused by the crime." The petitioner again appealed to the U.S. Supreme Court where the lower court's sentencing (but not the conviction) was vacated and remanded back for further proceedings.

The Supreme Court reversed Booth's death sentence, holding that it is cruel and unusual to let juries hear evidence about how a murder affected the victim's family.

Writing for the 5-4 majority of the Supreme Court, Justice Lewis F. Powell, Jr., said the jury's job in a death penalty case is to decide whether the criminal deserves to die based on his character and background and the circumstances of the murder. The jury is supposed to focus on the criminal's personal responsibility and moral guilt. Victim impact statements make the jury focus on the victim instead of the criminal. The decision found that introducing a VIS into jury deliberations during the sentencing phase of a capital murder trial posed a risk of overly prejudicing a jury and thus violated the Eighth Amendment. Writing for the majority, Justice Powell observed that in a capital case, the jury's sentencing task is based on consideration of a defendant as a unique individual. The focus of a VIS, however, was not on the defendant but on the victim's character and reputation and the effect of the crime on a victim's family. Justices agreed with Booth's attorney--the potential for admission of emotionally-charged opinions that might be presented in a VIS was irrelevant to sentencing deliberations because each family possesses a differing ability to show grief. Although the murder of the Bronsteins was a heinous crime, the Court held that, at the time of the crime, Booth was nonetheless unaware of potential consequences on the victims' family (or that the victims had a family) and such information would have been irrelevant in his decision to kill. Thus, such factors as contained in a VIS were inappropriate to consider during sentencing. The majority opinion further reasoned that the presentation of a VIS could cause a jury to divert from the relevant evidence of the crime. Ultimately, the Court held that admission of a VIS created a constitutionally unacceptable risk that the jury might impose the death penalty "in an arbitrary and capricious manner."[192]

The majority's holding was based on the assumption that VIS might tend to unduly influence juries, thus negatively influencing sentencing. Thus, the so-called playing field was not level.[193]

In a scathing dissenting opinion, Justice Scalia reflected what would, in later years, become an increasing social bias in favor of victim's rights over those of the accused. Dissenting justices felt that if punishment could be enhanced in non-capital cases on the basis of the harm caused (such as information of the kind provided in a VIS), then there was no reason why the majority opinion should have found the same

---

[192] *Booth v Maryland,* 482 US 496 (1987)
[193] O'Sullivan, Carol. *The Death Penalty: Identifying Propaganda Techniques.* San Diego: Greenhaven Press, 1989.

unconstitutional in capital cases. Moreover, justices felt that if the defendant was entitled to be considered as an individual, so too, the victim should have been considered an individual whose death represented a unique loss to family and society. Thus, the dissenting opinion concluded that the only proper basis for setting punishment was not merely the perpetrator's circumstances or frame of mind, but also the amount of harm inflicted on the victim.[194]

Initially the United States Supreme Court held that testimony in the form of a victim impact statement is only admissible during the sentencing phase of a trial if it directly relates to the "circumstances of the crime". In a majority opinion by Justice Brennan authored the opinion of the court. The Court held that *Booth v. Maryland* (1987) left open the possibility that the kind of information contained in victim impact statements could be admissible if it "relate[d] directly to the circumstances of the crime." Though South Carolina asserted that such is the case here, the Court disagreed, holding that the content of the cards at issue to be irrelevant to the "circumstances of the crime." Justice O'Connor authored a dissenting opinion, joined by Chief Justice Rehnquist and Justice Kennedy; Justice Scalia also dissented arguing that *Booth v. Maryland* must be overruled.[195]

Overturned it was just two years later. A Tennessee court tried Pervis Payne for murdering Charisse Christopher and her daughter Lacie. In hopes of avoiding the death penalty, Payne provided four witnesses testifying to his good character. The prosecution had Charisse's mother share how Charisse's death had impacted her surviving son Nicholas. In closing arguments, the prosecutor referenced Nicholas' loss of his mother when calling for the death penalty. The jury convicted him and sentenced him to death. Payne argued that the prosecution could not use testimony of how the victim's death impacted family members when contending for the death penalty. The Tennessee Supreme Court upheld the death sentence.

The case came to the U.S. Supreme Court on appeal. The appellant

---

[194] *Booth v Maryland,* 482 US 496 (1987)
[195] *South Carolina v. Gathers,* 490 U.S. 805 (1989)

asked if the Eighth Amendment prohibited a capital sentencing jury from considering the impact that a victim's death had upon surviving family members.

Writing for the Court, Chief Justice William H. Rehnquist answered in the negative delivering the opinion for a 6-3 divided court. The Chief Justice's opinion overruled *Booth v. Maryland* and *South Carolina v. Gathers* which prohibited the submission of evidence relating to the harms caused by the victim's death. The Court reasoned that since "[v]irtually no limits are placed on the relevant mitigating evidence a capital defendant may introduce concerning his own circumstances," the prosecution must be allowed to submit similar counter evidence. Evidence regarding the "assessment of the harm caused by the defendant has long been an important factor in determining the appropriate punishment, and victim impact evidence is simply another method of informing the sentencing authority about such harm."[196]

---

[196] *Payne v Tennessee*, 501 US 808 (1991)

# Capital Punishment
# and the Federal Government

It was inevitable that the national government, even in its weakest form known as the Articles of Confederation, would be forced to consider certain crimes subject of national jursidiction and thus punishment. Recalling that the first known execution in the New World was for treason, it was inevitable that one day the national government would have to act. Transgressions such as piracy were universally recognized as violations of the law of nations and thus required punishment by national, not territorial, governments. The new national government of the United States necessarily inherited responsibility for punishment of some crimes from the British government when we declared our independence. Many of these offenses against the national government were subject to capital punishment.

## Creating a National Judiciary

The Judiciary Act of 1789[197] was a landmark statute adopted on September 24, 1789 in the first session of the first Congress which established the national judiciary. The Constitution had merely prescribed that the "judicial power of the United States, shall be vested in one supreme Court," and such inferior courts as Congress saw fit to establish. It made no provision, though, for the composition or procedures of any of the courts, leaving this to Congress to decide. Before and after ratification,

---

[197] U.S. Judiciary Act of 1789; Act of Sept. 24, 1789, ch. 20, §9(b), 1 Stat. 79.10; Ch. 20, 1 Stat. 73

some opponents of a strong judiciary urged that the federal court system be limited to a Supreme Court and perhaps admiralty judges. The Congress, however, decided to establish a system of federal trial courts with broader jurisdiction, thereby creating an arm for enforcement of national laws within each state. The Judiciary Act was reported to the Senate by Senator Richard Henry Lee of Virginia on June 12, 1789. The main author of the bill was Senator Oliver Ellsworth of Connecticut.[198] The Act was passed by the Senate by a vote of 14 to 6 on July 17, 1789. The bill was debated by the House in July and August 1789 before being passed with amendments on September 17, 1789 by a vote of 37 to 16. The Senate agreed to all but four of the House's amendments on September 19, 1789. The House passed the bill as agreed to by Senate on September 21, 1789. On September 24, 1789, President Washington signed the Judiciary Act of 1789 into law.[199]

The Judiciary Act was an omnibus bill, having several objects, the most important of which was to create the federal judiciary. It set the number of Supreme Court justices as six [five associate justices and the Chief Justice]. It gave the Supreme Court original jurisdiction over all civil actions between states, or between a state and the United States and otherwise set the jurisdiction of the federal courts. It treated judicial districts for courts of original jurisdiction. The statute created the offices of Attorney General, U.S. Attorney and U.S. Marshal. The ACTA was almost an afterthought and between 1790 and 1980 was cited as establishing jurisdiction only twice and then for limited purposes.[200] House of Representatives. Madison had been the principal sponsor of the Judiciary Act in the House at the same time. Combined, the Judiciary Act and Bill of Rights gave the Constitution considerable power that had been missing in the Articles of Confederation. Judicial Review guaranteed the federal government's sovereignty, whereas the Bill of Rights guaranteed

---

[198] William R. Casto, *Oliver Ellsworth and the Creation of the Federal Republic.* New York: Second Circuit Committee on History and Commemorative Events, 1997.

[199] Information from the Library of Congress

[200] Hufbauer, Gary Clyde; Mitrokostas, Nicholas K. (2004). "International Implications of the Alien Tort Statute." 16 *St. Thomas L. Rev.* 607 at 609 (2004).

the protection of states and citizens from the misuse of this sovereignty by the federal government. The Judiciary Act and Bill of Rights thus counterbalanced each other, each guaranteeing respite from the excesses of the other.[201]

Oliver Ellsworth was ideally suited to serve as principal author of the Judiciary Act. Ellsworth (1745-1807) was born on 29 April 1745 in Windsor, Connecticut. He was a lawyer, a revolutionary against British rule, a member of the Continental Congress, and one of those who drafted the U. S. Constitution. At the Constitutional Convention Ellsworth played a major role in the passage of the Connecticut Plan. During debate he joined his fellow Connecticut delegate Roger Sherman (1721-1793) in proposing the two house [bicameral] arrangement in which members of the Senate would be elected by state legislatures. Ellsworth's version of the compromise was adopted by the Convention. Although Ellsworth left the Convention near the end of August and did not sign the final document, he wrote the Letters of a Landowner which promoted its ratification. He also played a dominant role in Connecticut's 1788 ratification convention, when he emphasized that judicial review guaranteed federal sovereignty. He served as a member of the Convention's Committee of Detail but never mentioned judicial review in the draft of the Constitution. Later, however, he did stress its central importance at the ratifying conventions.[202]

Ellsworth quickly won wide respect for his diligence, or, as one biographer has put it, "his recognition of the fact that in the senatorial office drudging spadework was even more important than speeches and votes." On July 17, 1789, the Senate enacted its version of this landmark statute. With House revisions, it became law two months later. Oliver Ellsworth remained a highly effective senator until 1796, when he moved to the Supreme Court as chief justice of the United States, serving as the third chief justice. Although Ellsworth, more than any other, shaped the

---

[201] See Rogers, John M., "The Alien Tort Statute and How Individuals Violate International Law," 21 *Vand. J. Transnat'l Law* 47 (1988). Rogers offers an excellent summary of the purpose of the first Congress.

[202] Casto, William R., *The Supreme Court in the Early Republic: The Chief Justiceships of John Jay and Oliver Ellsworth*, University of South Carolina Press, 1995

federal judicial system, his strengths as a legislative craftsman failed to translate to success as a jurist. Deteriorating health forced his resignation within four years.

Ellsworth was a student and intellectual heir of Emmerich de Vattel (1714-1767). Vattel, in turn, was the heir of the legal tradition of Hugo de Groot (1585-1645), commonly known as Grotius. Both Grotius and Vattel discerned the principles of natural law from and by reason rather than from reliance on God and theology. Vattel published his Law of Nations[203] in 1758 and it was widely read and accepted in America. Just as lawyers read William Blackstone's work on English law so many Founding Fathers read and applied Vattel's ideas. The decisive influence of Vattel's classic study may be attributed to its eclecticism. Vattel rejected the extreme claims of the natural law of nations which went back to Thomas Aquinas (1225-1274). Instead, he recognized that the universal law of nature might have subsidiary force when customary or consensual international law was silent. *Le Droit de Gens* was a legal work of the first magnitude for it modernized the whole theory of International Law, brought it out of philosophical study into practical reality. Vattel accomplished much for nations, for he imposed upon them theories of moral rational development which were necessary for them to co-exist with other nations. Just as other early Americans had relied on Vattel to guidec them in formulating the U.S. Constitution so Ellsworth relied upon Vattel to create a modern judiciary.

Ellsworth's s Senate colleagues had also selected him to chair a committee to draft the chamber's rules of pro-cedure. Ellsworth quickly won wide respect for his diligence, or, as one biographer has put it, "his recognition of the fact that in the senatorial office drudging spadework was even more important than speeches and votes." On July 17, 1789, the Senate enacted its version of this landmark statute. With House revisions, it became law two months later.

---

[203] The whole title of Vattel's work is: *The Law of Nations; Or, Principles of the Law of Nature, Applied to the Conduct and Affairs of Nations and Sovereigns. A Work Tending to Display the True Interest of Powers.*

# The Crimes Act of 1790

The Crimes Act of 1790, also known as the Federal Criminal Code of 1790, was formally titled An Act for the Punishment of Certain Crimes Against the United States. The law defined some of the first federal crimes in the United States and expanded on the criminal procedure provisions of the Judiciary Act of 1789. The U.S. Constitution had left the Congress to establish the full jurisdiction, composition, and nature of the federal court system.

The Crimes Act was a "comprehensive statute defining an impressive variety of federal crimes." It defined certain capital offenses, namely: treason, murder, robbery, piracy, mutiny, hostility against the United States, counterfeiting, and aiding the escape of a capital prisoner. As an enactment of the First Congress, the Crimes Act is often regarded as a quasi-constitutional text. The punishment of treason, piracy, counterfeiting, as well as crimes committed on the high seas or against the law of nations, followed from relatively explicit constitutional authority. The creation of crimes within areas under exclusive federal jurisdiction followed from the plenary power of Congress over the "Seat of the Government," federal enclaves, and federal territories. The creation of crimes involving the integrity of the judicial process derived from Congress's authority to establish such courts.

The Crimes Act also established a statute of limitations for federal crimes, provided for criminal venue, ensured procedural protections for treason and capital defendants, simplified the pleading requirements for perjury, and broadened the constitutional protection against "corruption of blood." Further, the act provided for punitive dissection of murderers and codified diplomatic immunity.

# Federal Executions

The first federal execution was that of Thomas Bird on June 25, 1790 due to his committing "murder on the high seas. From 1790 to 1963, there were 340 Federal, 271 Territorial and 40 Indian Tribunal executions according to the most complete records. One of those was the execution of James Arcene on June 18, 1885, at the age of 23 for his role in a robbery and murder committed when he was 10 years old. Between 1950 and 1963,

13 people were executed, not counting those executed under military law.

In the late 1980s, Senator Alfonse D'Amato, from New York State, sponsored a bill to make certain federal drug crimes eligible for the death penalty as he was disgusted by the failure of his home state to enact death penalty legislation. The Anti-Drug Abuse Act of 1988 restored the death penalty under federal law for drug offenses and some types of murder. President Bill Clinton signed the Violent Crime Control and Law Enforcement Act, expanding the federal death penalty in 1994. In response to the Oklahoma City bombing, the Antiterrorism and Effective Death Penalty Act of 1996 was enacted.

Presently, capital punishment at the federal level can be handed down for treason, espionage, murder, large-scale drug trafficking, or attempted murder of a witness, juror, or court officer in certain cases. Twenty-six federal executions, including military executions, have been carried out since 1950. Three executions, none of them military, have occurred since the reinstatement of capital punishment. This list only includes those executed under federal jurisdiction. Since 1963, three people have been executed by the federal government of the United States.[204] All were executed by lethal injection at U.S. Prison at Terre Haute, Indiana.[205]

By far the best known federal execution was of Timothy James McVeigh (1968–2001). He was an American domestic terrorist who perpetrated the 1995 Oklahoma City bombing, which killed 168 people and injured over 680 others. The bombing was the deadliest act of domestic terrorism within the United States in United States history. McVeigh sought revenge against the federal government for the three incidents: the 1993 Waco siege, which ended in the deaths of 86 people,

[204] *Gregg v. Georgia, Proffitt v. Florida, Jurek v. Texas, Woodson v. North Carolina,* and *Roberts v. Louisiana,* 428 U.S. 153 (1976).

[205] Brigham, John. "Unusual Punishment: The Federal Death Penalty in the United States." *Washington University Journal of Law & Policy*. January 2004. Volume 16 (Access to Justice: The Social Responsibility of Lawyers | New Federalism). p. 195-233. See also Tirschwell, Eric A. and Theodore Hertzberg. "Politics and Prosecutions: A Historical Perspective on Shifting Federal Standards for Pursuing the Death Penalty in non-Death Penalty States." *Journal of Constitutional Law*. October 2009. Volume 12 Issue 1. p. 57-98.

many of whom were children, and which occurred exactly two years before the bombing; the 1992 Ruby Ridge incident which began on August 21, 1992, and which resulted in a shootout and the deaths of Deputy US Marshal William Francis Degan, age 42; Weaver's 43-year-old wife Vicki who was killed by FBI sniper fire; and certain aspects of the United States foreign policy. Reportedly, McVeigh hoped to inspire a revolt against the federal government. He defended the bombing as a legitimate tactic against what he saw as a tyrannical federal government. He was quickly arrested after the bombing and indicted for eleven federal offenses, including the use of a weapon of mass destruction. He was found guilty on all counts in 1997 and sentenced to death. McVeigh's death sentence was delayed pending an appeal. One of his appeals for certiorari, taken to the Supreme Court of the United States, was denied on March 8, 1999. McVeigh's request for a nationally televised execution was also denied. An Internet company also unsuccessfully sued for the right to broadcast his execution. McVeigh dropped his remaining appeals, saying that he would rather die than spend the rest of his life in prison. On January 16, 2001 the Federal Bureau of Prisons set May 16, 2001, as McVeigh's execution date. McVeigh stated that his only regret was not completely destroying the federal building. Six days prior to his scheduled execution, the FBI turned over thousands of documents of evidence to McVeigh's; lawyers, documents it had previously withheld. As a result, U.S. Attorney General John Ashcroft announced McVeigh's execution would be stayed for one month. The execution date was reset for June 11, 2001. McVeigh requested a Catholic chaplain and two pints of mint chocolate chip ice cream for his last meal.[206]

Juan Raul Garza (1957 –2001) was an American murderer and drug trafficker who was executed for a federal crime. In 1993, Garza was convicted of murdering three people while running a marijuana smuggling and distribution ring based in Brownsville, Texas. He was sentenced to

---

[206] Most conveniently and fully covered by Wikipedia. See also Jones, Stephen and Peter Israel. *Others Unknown: Timothy McVeigh and the Oklahoma City Bombing Conspiracy*, 2nd ed. New York: PublicAffairs, 2001; and Madeira, Jody Lyneé. *Killing McVeigh: The Death Penalty and the Myth of Closure*. New York University Press, 2012.

death and appealed on the basis that the jury were allegedly not told that they had the power to recommend life imprisonment instead of the death sentence. Garza's lawyers also claimed that it was unfair that the jury were told that Garza was suspected of four murders in Mexico given that, although a prime suspect in these crimes, he had never been charged with, or convicted of them.

The attorneys appealed to the Inter-American Commission on Human Rights, an independent human rights body of the Organization of American States (OAS). On December 4, 2000, the Commission transmitted to the U. S. State Department a merits report stated that: "the Commission considers that the State's conduct in introducing evidence of un-adjudicated foreign crimes during Mr. Garza's capital sentencing hearing was antithetical to the most basic and fundamental judicial guarantees applicable in attributing responsibility and punishment to individuals for crimes. Accordingly, the Commission finds that the State is responsible for imposing the death penalty upon Mr. Garza in a manner contrary to his right to a fair trial under Article XVIII of the American Declaration, as well as his right to due process of law under Article XXVI of the Declaration. . . ."

The State Department ignored the OAS and all other appeals failed. On June 19, 2001, Garza was executed at the Federal Correctional Complex, Terre Haute by lethal injection.[207]

The Federal Bureau of Prisons manages the housing and execution of federal death row prisoners. As of September 28, 2018, 63 offenders were on the federal death row, most of them at Federal Correctional Complex in Terre Haute, Indiana. Executions are carried out by lethal injections.

## Execution for Espionage

Julius and Ethel Rosenberg were American citizens who committed espionage on behalf of the Soviet Union and against their own nation. They were tried, convicted, and executed by the federal government of the United States. They provided top-secret information

---

[207] Wikipedia entry for Juan Raul Garza.

about radar, sonar, and jet propulsion engines to the USSR and were accused of transmitting valuable nuclear weapon designs to the Soviet Union; at that time the United States was the only country in the world with nuclear weapons.

Born in New York of Jewish immigrant parents Julius was an early leader of the Young Communist League at the City College of New York. Ethel Greenglass was also born into a Jewish family in New City. After failing as a singer and actress she joined the Young Communist League where in 1936 she met and then married Julius Rosenberg in 1939.

On March 29, 1951, the Rosenberg's were convicted of espionage. They were sentenced to death on April 5 by Judge Kaufman, which prohibits transmitting or attempting to transmit to a foreign government information "relating to the national defense".[208] In imposing the death penalty, Judge Kaufman had this to say:

> I consider your crime worse than murder . . . I believe your conduct in putting into the hands of the Russians the A-Bomb years before our best scientists predicted Russia would perfect the bomb has already caused, in my opinion, the Communist aggression in Korea, with the resultant casualties exceeding 50,000 and who knows but that millions more of innocent people may pay the price of your treason. Indeed, by your betrayal you undoubtedly have altered the course of history to the disadvantage of our country. No one can say that we do not live in a constant state of tension. We have evidence of your treachery all around us every day for the civilian defense activities throughout the nation are aimed at preparing us for an atom bomb attack.[209]

The United States government did not operate an execution chamber at the time when the Rosenberg's were sentenced to death. They were transferred to New York State's Sing Sing Correctional Facility in

---

[208] Section 2 of the Espionage Act of 1917, 50 U.S. Code 32 (now 18 U.S. Code 794).

[209] "Judge Kaufman's Statement Upon Sentencing the Rosenbergs". University of Missouri–Kansas City. Archived from the original. This statement in widely quoted and reprinted in most books and articles on the Rosenberg Trial.

Ossining, New York, for execution. Julius and Ethel Rosenberg were electrocuted by executioner Joseph Francel at sundown on June 19, 1953, with a modification made in respect for the Jewish Sabbath.

Others convicted included Ethel's brother, David Greenglass, who stole documents from Los Alamos; Harry Gold, who was the courier for Greenglass; Klaus Fuchs, a scientist working in Los Alamos who was handled by Gold. As time passed and Soviet archives were opened researchers discovered that Fuchs provided vastly more important information to the Soviets than did the Rosenberg's. [210] Fuchs was convicted in Great Britain and served nine years and four months in prison. Researchers also discovered that Greenglass was far more important than thought at the time of the Rosenberg's' trial. [211]

Protests against the impending executions were led by French Marxist Jean Paul Sartre, and included many international notables of the far left of the political spectrum. Hollywood's leftist activists predictably joined in. [212] Other non-communist notables, including the Roman Catholic Pope, filed appeals for clemency. [213]

For decades the Rosenberg children and many others on the political left bemoaned their execution. However, files in the Soviet archives proved Julius's role as a courier and recruiter for the Soviets and Ethel's role as an accessory. Five historians who have published works based on the Rosenberg case all agreed that Soviet documents show that Ethel Rosenberg hid money and espionage paraphernalia for Julius, served as an intermediary for communications with his Soviet intelligence contacts, relayed her personal evaluation of individuals whom Julius considered recruiting, and was present at meetings with his sources.

Many historians, again largely, but not exclusively, drawn from the communists and their allies, have claimed that the execution of the

---

[210] Hornblum, Allen M. *The Invisible Harry Gold: The Man Who Gave the Soviets the Atom Bomb.* Yale University Press 2010.

[211] Carmichael, Virginia. *Framing History: the Rosenberg Story and the Cold War.* University of Minnesota Press, 1993.

[212] Aftalion, Florin. *La Trahison des Rosenberg*, Paris: J.C. Lattès, 2003.

[213] https://www.history.com/this-day-in-history/julius-and-ethel-rosenberg-executed. See also A&E Television network special on the Rosenberg Trial.

Rosenberg's was caused primarily by Cold War hysteria, exacerbated by the ongoing Korean Police Action. In more normal times, they argue, executions would have been reduced to imprisonment.[214] To others on the political right, were that so, the United States might well have executed Greenglass and sought the extradition and subsequent execution of Fuchs.

In refusing clemency, then President Dwight D. Eisenhower mentioned the deaths of millions that were caused by the Rosenberg's' spying. The deaths of two persons was a matter of grave concern, the President said, but paled in comparison to the harm done by their espionage.

## Military Executions

Following the American Civil War Dr. Henry Wirz (1823-1865), commandant of Andersonville Prison where the Confederacy held thousands of Union Soldiers, was tried for war crimes. Because of the rapid increase in the number of prisoners the Confederate government decided to build Andersonville Prison in Georgia. In April 1864 Winder appointed Wirz as commandant of this new prison camp. By August, 1864, there were 32,000 Union Army prisoners in Andersonville. The Confederate authorities did not provide enough food for the prison and men began to die of starvation. The water became polluted and disease was a constant problem. Of the 49,485 prisoners who entered the camp, nearly 13,000 died from disease and malnutrition. The Union tried Wirz on the charge of "conspiring to injure the health and destroy the lives of United States soldiers held as prisoners by the Confederate States". Wirz appeared before a military commission headed by Major General Lew Wallace on 21st August, 1865. During the trial a letter from Wirz was presented that showed that he had complained to his superiors about the shortage of food being provided for the prisoners. However, former inmates at Andersonville testified that Wirz inspected the prison every day and often warned that if any man escaped he would "starve every damn Yankee for it." The tribunal found Wirz guilty and sentenced to death. He

---

[214] For example, Clune, Lori, *Executing the Rosenbergs: Death and Diplomacy in a Cold War World* Oxford University Press, 2016. Clune is associate professor of history at California State University, Fresno.

was taken to Washington to be executed on November 10, 1865. The gallows were surrounded by Union Army soldiers who throughout the procedure chanted "Wirz, remember, Andersonville." Accompanied by a Catholic priest, Wirz refused to make a last minute confession, claiming he was not guilty of committing any crime. Major Russell read the death warrant and then told Wirz he "deplored this duty." Wirz replied that: "I know what orders are, Major. And I am being hanged for obeying them." Dr. Wirz claimed that he merely acted as a subordinate in carrying out the orders of the commander of the post. The Judge Advocate General admitted that indeed Dr. Wirz had acted under orders, but responded, "A superior officer cannot order a subordinate to do an illegal act, and if a subordinate obey such an order and disastrous consequences result, both the superior and the subordinate must answer for it. General Winder could no more command the prisoner to violate the laws of war than could the prisoner do so without orders."[215]

The United States military has executed 135 people since 1916. The most recent person to be executed by the military is U.S. Army Private John A. Bennett, executed on April 13, 1961 for rape and attempted murder. Since the end of the Civil War in 1865, only one person has been executed for a purely military offense: Private Eddie Slovik, who was executed on January 31, 1945 after being convicted of desertion.

Over 21,000 American soldiers were given varying sentences for desertion during World War II, including forty-nine death sentences, Slovik's death sentence was the only one that was actually carried out. During World War II, 1.7 the U.S. military conducted over a million courts-martial. That represented approximately one third of all criminal cases tried in the United States during the same period. Most of the cases were minor, and the sentences were light. In 1945 the Secretary of War appointed a clemency board which reviewed all general courts-martial where the accused was still in confinement, and remitted or reduced the sentence in 85 percent of the 27,000 cases reviewed. The military rarely

---

[215] The Trial of Henry Wirz, A Congressionally Mandated Report Summarizing the Military Commission's Proceedings, United States. 40th Congress, 2d Session. 1867–1868. House Executive Document No. 23, December 7, 1867.

imposed the death penalty and then primarily for rapes or murders. In the Oise-Aisne American Cemetery and Memorial in Fère-en-Tardenois alone, there are buried 95 American soldiers executed for rape or murder – and Eddie Slovik.

Slovik was the only soldier executed who had been convicted of a "purely military" offense. General Dwight Eisenhower confirmed the execution order on December 23, noting that it was necessary to discourage further desertions. The sentence came as a shock to Slovik, who had expected to receive only a dishonorable discharge and perhaps a prison term. Such was the punishment he had seen meted out to other deserters from the division. Because he was an ex-convict, a dishonorable discharge would have had little additional impact on his civilian life. Moreover, it was widely expected that military prison terms for virtually all soldiers convicted of disciplinary offenses would commuted once the war was over.

Execution by firing squad was carried out at 10:04 a.m. on January 31, 1945, near the village of Sainte-Marie-aux-Mines. The unrepentant Slovik related to the soldiers whose duty it was to prepare him for the firing squad that it was his belief that he was being executed as an example only because he had a prior minor criminal record.

The United States joined with the other allied powers following the end of World War II to try the major German and Japanese leaders in international courts staffed by civilians. Each allied nation was also free to try any other war criminals. The conviction of Japanese Generals Yamashita and Hirota took place in the war-torn Philippines. Lawyers for these men appealed their conviction to the United States Supreme Court seeking a writ of habeas corpus. The Supreme Court held that the military tribunal set up in Japan by General MacArthur as the agent of the Allied Powers is not a tribunal of the United States, and the courts of the United States have no power or authority to review, affirm, set aside, or annul the judgments and sentences imposed by it on these petitioners, all of whom are residents and citizens of Japan.[216] The

---

[216] *Hirota v MacArthur*, 338 U. S. 198 (1949).Together with No. 240, Misc., *Dohihara v. MacArthur, General of the Army, et al.* and No. 248, Misc. *Kido*

case was argued on 16 and 17 December 1949.

The high court ruled that the petitioners, all residents and citizens of Japan, were being held in custody pursuant to the judgments of a military tribunal in Japan. Two of the petitioners have been sentenced to death, the others to terms of imprisonment. They filed motions in the Supreme Court for leave to file petitions for habeas corpus. The high court set all the motions for hearing on the question of our power to grant the relief prayed,[217] and that issue has now been fully presented and argued. It was satisfied that the tribunal sentencing these petitioners is not a tribunal of the United States. The United States and other allied countries conquered and now occupy and control Japan. General Douglas MacArthur has been selected and is acting as the Supreme Commander for the Allied Powers. The military tribunal sentencing these petitioners has been set up by General MacArthur as the agent of the Allied Powers. Under the foregoing circumstances, the courts of the United States have no power or authority to review, to affirm, set aside, or annul the judgments and sentences imposed on these petitioners, and, for this reason, the motions for leave to file petitions for writs of habeas corpus are denied.[218]

Justice Douglas wrote a concurring opinion in which he argued that "If an American General holds a prisoner, our process can reach him wherever he is. To that extent at least the Constitution follows the flag. It is no defense for him to say that the acts for the Allied Powers. He is an American citizen who is performing functions for our government. It is our Constitution which he supports and defends. If there is evasion or violation of its obligations, it is no defense that he acts for another nation. There is at present no group or confederation to which an official of this Nation owes a higher obligation than he owes to us."

The case was of some interest in a later decision. In March 2008, the U.S. government cited *Hirota v. MacArthur* as "directly applicable" in

---

*et al. v. MacArthur, General of the Army, et al.,*
[217] 335 U. S. 876
[218] Snell, Willis B., "Habeas Corpus—Jurisdiction of Federal Courts to Review Jurisdiction of Military Tribunals When the Prisoner Is Physically Confined outside the United States". *Michigan Law Review.* 49 (6): 870–881 (April 1951).

a case regarding defendants held in Iraq. Shawqi Omar and Mohammad Munaf were American citizens who voluntarily traveled to Iraq and allegedly committed crimes there. They were each captured by military forces. They were given hearings before Tribunals composed of American officers, which concluded that petitioners posed threats to Iraq's security; and placed in the custody of the U. S. The government argued before the Supreme Court that U.S. federal courts lacked jurisdiction over two U.S. citizens being held by the military in Iraq and thus could not review their petitions for habeas corpus.[219]

One recent military execution involved rape and murder. On February 18, 1995, Louis Jones Jr., a former soldier, kidnapped, raped and murdered Army soldier Tracie Joy McBride. Jones kidnapped Private McBride, a 19-year old from Centerville, Minnesota. Supposedly, Jones was looking for his wife, but instead decided to kidnap McBride. McBride was on the telephone with a friend in a laundry facility when she was abducted. Two privates attempted to rescue McBride, but Jones thwarted the effort. Jones took McBride to his house, raped her, and held her in a closet. Jones attempted to conceal the crime in various ways. He then drove McBride to a remote area and beat her to death with a tire iron. Jones was tried and convicted in the U.S. federal court system. Jones, sentenced to death because he had also raped her, argued that he should be spared the death penalty due to the damages he received from the "Gulf War syndrome." His appeals were unsuccessful and he was put to death by lethal injection in 2003.

## Presidential Assassins

Until the assassination of President John Kennedy in 1963 there was no federal law under which an assassin could be tried. The trial of the Lincoln conspirators was held in a special military tribunal and followed brutal procedures under martial law. It found guilty and executed under martial law Lewis Powell, David Herold, George Atzerodt, and Mary Surratt.[220]

---

[219] Munaf v. Geren, 553 U.S. 674 (2008)

[220] Speed, Attorney General James, *Opinion on the constitutional power of the military to try and execute the assassins of the President.* Washington:

Secretary of War Edwin Stanton favored a quick military trial and execution. According to Secretary of Navy Gideon Welles, who favored trial in a civilian court, Stanton "said it was intention that the criminals should be tried and executed before President Lincoln was buried." As it was, Lincoln was buried on May 4, that is, before the start of the conspiracy trial. Edward Bates, Lincoln's former attorney general, was among those objecting to a military trial, believing such an approach to be unconstitutional.

Understanding the use of a military commission to try civilians to be controversial, President Johnson requested Attorney General James Speed to prepare an opinion on the legality of such a trial. Not surprisingly, Speed concluded in his opinion that use of a military court would be proper. Speed reasoned that an attack on the commander-in-chief before the full cessation of the rebellion constituted an act of war against the United States, making the War Department the appropriate body to control the proceedings.

While debates continued in the Johnson Administration as to how to proceed with the alleged conspirators, the prisoners were kept under close wraps at two locations. Mary Surratt and Dr. Samuel Mudd were jailed initially at the Old Capitol Prison, while the other six were imprisoned on the ironclad vessels *Montauk* and *Saugus*. Later, as their trial date approached, authorities confined prisoners to separate cells in the Old Arsenal Penitentiary. Four of the male prisoners--Herold, Powell, Spangler, and Atzerodt--were shackled to balls and chains, with their hands held in place by an inflexible iron bar. Most strikingly, from the time of their arrest until midway through their trial, all the prisoners except Mary Surratt and Dr. Mudd--under orders from Secretary Stanton--were forced to wear canvas hoods that covered the entire head and face.

On May 1, 1865, President Johnson issued an order that the alleged conspirators be tried before a nine-person military commission.

---

Government Printing Office, 1865; *The assassination of Abraham Lincoln, late President of the United States of America and the attempted assassination of William H. Seward, Secretary of State, and Frederick W. Seward, Assistant Secretary, on the evening of the 14th of April, 1865.* Washington: Government Printing Office, 1867.

Some, such as former Attorney General Bates, complained bitterly: "If the offenders are done to death by that tribunal, however truly guilty, they will pass for martyrs with half the world."

The Military Commission convened for the first time on May 8 in a newly-created courtroom on the third floor of the Old Arsenal Penitentiary in Washington. The voting members of the Commission were Generals David Hunter, August Kautz, Albion Howe, James Ekin, David Clendenin, Lewis Wallace, Robert Foster, T. M. Harris, and Colonel C. H Tomkins. Judge Advocate General Joseph Holt served in the dual roles of chief prosecutor and legal adviser to the Commission. John A. Bingham served on the Commission as Special Judge Advocates and handled examination of witnesses and gave the government's summation. H. L. Burnett was the third member of the prosecution team.

The connection of Lewis Powell and David Herold to the conspiracy was clear beyond question. The case against others was considerably more circumstantial, but nonetheless ultimately convincing. Michael O'Laughlen was assigned to kill Staunton but got drunk instead. George Atzerodt was supposed to kill Vice-president Andrew Johnson. By any reasonable standard the cases against Dr. Samuel Mudd and Mary Surratt were at best tenuous. President Johnson considered Mary Surratt the "nest that hatched the plot." Moreover, she had guns that supposedly belonged to the conspirators.

Mary Surratt, Lewis Powell, George Atzerodt, and David Herold) were sentenced "to be hanged by the neck until he [or she] be dead." Samuel Arnold, Dr. Samuel Mudd and Michael O'Laughlen were sentenced to "hard labor for life, at such place at the President shall direct." Edman Spangler received a six-year sentence. On July 5, Andrew Johnson approved all of the Commission's sentences, including the death sentence for Surratt.

The next day General Hartrandft informed the prisoners of their sentences. He told the four condemned prisoners that they would hang the next day. Mrs. Surratt's lawyers mounted a frantic effort to save their client's life, hurriedly preparing a petition for *habeas corpus* that evening. The next morning, Surratt's attorneys succeeded in convincing Judge Wylie of the Court of the District of Columbia to issue the requested writ.

President Johnson quashed the effort to save Surratt from an afternoon hanging when he issued an order suspending the writ of habeas corpus "in cases such as this." Shortly after one-thirty on the afternoon of July 7, 1865, the trap of the gallows installed in the courtyard of the Old Arsenal Building was sprung, and the four condemned prisoners fell to their deaths.[221]

The clearly extra-legal way the trial of the Lincoln Conspirators remains a blot on the federal government. In its own way it was nearly as notorious as the assassination.

The assassination of President James Garfield were prosecuted by the federal government because they took place in the District of Columbia. Charles Guiteau's trial was held in D.C. court the assassin of William McKinley, Leon Czolgosz, was tried and executed for murder by New York state authorities.

---

[221] Steers Jr., Edward, and Holzer, Harold, eds. *The Lincoln Assassination Conspirators: Their Confinement and Execution, as Recorded in the Letterbook of John Frederick Hartranft*. Louisiana State University Press, 2009; Edwards, William C.; Steers, Edward, eds. *The Lincoln Assassination: The Evidence*. University of Illinois Press, 2010.

# Legal Methods of Execution

The great Roman philosopher and Emperor Marcus Aurelius Antoninus Augustus (121—180) in his *Meditations* observed, "Every Life ends in an execution. It is merely that some are more dreadful than others." The United States remains on a quest to find the least painful and presumably most merciful, method of executing condemned criminals. In this consideration we have followed closely that most approved studies of the methods of imposing the death penalty allowed by law in the United States.[222]

While in the beginning the primary concern of the drafters was to proscribe torture and other barbarous methods of punishment,[223] human perception of what constitutes cruel and unusual punishment has evolved.

While methods of execution have changed over the years, the U.S. Supreme Court noted that it "has never invalidated a State's chosen procedure for carrying out a sentence of death as the infliction of cruel and

---

[222] Weisberg, J. "This is Your Death," *The New Republic*, July 1, 1991. See also R. Bohm, R. *Deathquest: An Introduction to the Theory and Practice of Capital Punishment in the United States.* Anderson Publishing, 1999; Ecenbarger, W. "Perfecting Death: When the state kills it must do so humanely. Is that possible?," *Philadelphia Inquirer Magazine*, January 23, 1994; "Executions: Preparing Staff for the Hard Task Ahead," *Corrections Professional*, Vol. 1, February 16, 1996; and Hillman, H. "The Possible Pain Experienced During Executions by Different Methods," *Perception* 22: 745 (1992).

[223] Granucci, "Nor Cruel and Unusual Punishment Inflicted: The Original Meaning," 57 *Cal. L. Rev.* 839 (1969)], at 842.

unusual punishment."[224] We have therefore chosen to look at decisions from the highest courts in several states. These decisions have had a great bearing on practices of other states.

In a recent ruling the U.S. Supreme Court has held that challenges to the method of execution must be made in a particular way using a very old statute. United States Code section 1983 is the product of post-Civil War Republican reaction against the Ku Klux Klan. It was designed to provide civil action for deprivation of rights. President U. S. Grant asked for this legislation soon after he assumed the presidency. It was best known as The Enforcement Act of 1871,[225] but also known as the Civil Rights Act of 1871, Force Act of 1871, Ku Klux Klan Act, Third Enforcement Act, or Third Ku Klux Klan Act. Grant had been receiving of widespread racial threats in the Deep South, particularly in South Carolina. After the enactment of this law, the KKK was completely dismantled and did not resurface in any meaningful way until the first part of the 20th century. In the nearly 140 years since its passage the statute has been subject to only minor changes since then, but has been the subject of voluminous interpretation by courts. In its most recent form the act reads:

> Every person who under color of any statute, ordinance, regulation, custom, or usage, of any State or Territory or the District of Columbia, subjects, or causes to be subjected, any citizen of the United States or other person within the jurisdiction thereof to the deprivation of any rights, privileges, or immunities secured by the Constitution and laws, shall be liable to the party injured in an action at law, Suit in equity, or other proper proceeding for redress, except that in any action brought against a judicial officer for an act or omission taken in such officer's judicial capacity, injunctive relief shall not be granted unless a declaratory decree was violated or declaratory relief was unavailable. For the purposes of this section, any Act of Congress applicable exclusively to the District of Columbia shall be considered to be a

---

[224] *Baze v. Rees,* 553 U.S. 35 at 44 (2008)
[225] The Enforcement Act of 1871 (17 Stat. 13)

statute of the District of Columbia.[226]

In 2006 a case emanating from Florida[227] challenged the use of lethal injection as a form of execution in the state of Florida. The Court ruled unanimously that a challenge to the method of execution alleging violating the Eighth Amendment to the United States Constitution properly raised a claim under 42 U.S.C. § 1983, which provides a cause of action for civil rights violations, rather than under the *habeas corpus* provisions.

## Execution by Hanging

Once the overwhelming choice in both state and federal executions, hanging is now an allowable secondary method of execution in Delaware, New Hampshire and Washington, hanging was the primary method of execution used in the United States. Technically hanging is still the primary method of execution used in Delaware and Washington, although neither has executed a prisoner by hanging in many years. Both have lethal injection as an alternative method of execution.

For execution by this method, the inmate may be weighed the day before the execution, and a rehearsal is done using a sandbag of the same weight as the prisoner. This is to determine the length of drop necessary to ensure a quick death. If the rope is too long, the inmate could be decapitated, and if it is too short, the strangulation could occur, prolonging death to as long as 45 minutes. The rope, which should be 3/4-inch to 1 1/4-inch in diameter, is boiled and stretched to eliminate spring or coiling. The knot should be lubricated with wax or soap to ensure a smooth sliding action. The prisoner's hands and legs are secured, he is blindfolded, and the noose is placed around the neck, with the knot behind the left ear. The attendant opens a trap-door and the prisoner falls through. The prisoner's weight should cause a rapid fracture-dislocation of the neck. However, instantaneous death rarely occurs. If the inmate has strong neck muscles, is very light, if the drop is too short, or the noose has been wrongly positioned, the fracture-dislocation may not occur and death results from

---

[226] 42 U.S.C. § 1983
[227] *Hill v. McDonough,* 547 U.S. 573 (2006)

slow asphyxiation. If this occurs the face becomes engorged, the tongue protrudes, the eyes pop, the body defecates, and violent movements of the limbs occur.

Public hangings were common during the early part of the nineteenth century with the same lesson on morality being the reason for openness. In the new republic persons were no longer hanged for moral offenses such as adultery and witchcraft. By 1794 Pennsylvania hanged only criminals convicted of murder in the first degree. New York reduced the number of capital crimes from nineteen to two. Soon other states like Vermont, Virginia, Kentucky, Maryland, New Hampshire, and Ohio also had dramatically decreased the number of capital offenses. A few states actually moved in the opposite direction. Most of the southern states in addition to Rhode Island, Massachusetts, New Jersey, and Connecticut actually raised their number of capital offenses.

In 1936 when Rainey Bethea was hanged for rape, some 20,000 people came to Owensboro, Kentucky, to witness his execution. Bethea was the last individual to be hanged publicly in the United States. Hangings generally were discontinued as the method of execution soon after the end of World War II with only a very few used after 1950. Technically several states have retained hangings as an alternative method of execution should the primary method not be available for whatever reason.

One state court found hanging to be an unconstitutional method of execution.[228] In a Washington state case the defendants contended that execution by hanging violates the Eighth Amendment to the United States Constitution and Constitution, Article 1,14. The court began its consideration by emphasizing that the issue was not the constitutionality of the death penalty *per se* but only whether a particular method of executing the death penalty violates the constitution.

In defense of execution by hanging, the State cited a number of cases upholding the constitutionality of hanging as a means of execution. The court immediately recognized that these cases without exception were more than 50 years old, thus applying "long discarded standards" for

---

[228] *State v. Frampton,* 95 Wash. 2d 469, 627 P.2d 922, 934-35 (1981)

determining cruel and unusual punishment.[229] In another defense the state simply failed to discuss any standards, citing a 1951 Oregon case which does not even discuss the constitutionality of death by hanging.[230] On the other hand, the State cited no modern authority which held execution by hanging is constitutional.

## Lethal Gas

Commonly called the gas chamber, this method of execution is allowed, but is secondary to lethal injection, in these states: Alabama, Arizona, California, Mississippi, Missouri, Oklahoma and Wyoming. The last use of a gas chamber was on March 3, 1999, when Walter LaGrand, a German national, was executed in Arizona.

Execution by the use of cyanide gas was also introduced as a more humane way of executing inmates. Today, five states authorize lethal gas as a method of execution, but all have lethal injection as an alternative method. For execution by this method, the condemned person is strapped to a chair in an airtight chamber. A pail of sulfuric acid is placed beneath the chair. A long stethoscope is typically affixed to the inmate so that an attending physician outside the chamber can pronounce the prisoner dead. The room is sealed and an attendant pulls a lever that releases crystals of sodium cyanide into the pail. This causes a chemical reaction that releases hydrogen cyanide gas. The warden instructs the prisoner to breathe deeply to speed up the process and reduce pain. Most prisoners, however, try to hold their breath, and some struggle. The inmate does not lose consciousness immediately. According to former San Quenton, California, Penitentiary warden, Clifton Duffy, "At first there is evidence of extreme horror, pain, and strangling. The eyes pop. The skin turns purple and the victim begins to drool." Mass murderer Caryl Chessman, before he died in California's gas chamber in 1960 told reporters that he would nod his head if it hurt. Witnesses said he nodded his head for several minutes. Attendants use an exhaust fan to suction the poison air out of the chamber, and then they spray the corpse with ammonia to neutralize any remaining traces of cyanide. About a half an hour later, orderlies enter the chamber,

[229] *State v. Burris*, 194 Iowa 628, 190 N.W. 38 (1922)
[230] *State v. Leland,* 190 Ore. 598, 227 P.2d 785 (1951)

wearing gas masks and rubber gloves.

The case of *Fierro v. Gomez was decided in* October 1994. A U.S. District judge, Northern District (San Francisco), ruled the use of cyanide gas constituted cruel and unusual punishment and barred the state from using that method of execution. The lawsuit challenging the state's use of the gas chamber was filed by Robert Alton Harris and two other inmates on April 17, 1992, four days before Harris was scheduled to die. In the case of Robert Harris, the trial judge sentenced him as follows: "it is the Judgment and sentence of the Court with reference to Counts Five and Six of the Amended Information, that Robert Alton Harris shall be put to death by the administration of lethal gas within the walls of the State Prison at San Quentin, California. . . ." The California Supreme Court dismissed the suit, and Harris was put to death, marking the first execution in California in 25 years. California is one of only five states which, at that time, still employed the gas chamber as a method of execution the rest of the states have only lethal injection. Soon after the execution of Harris, the California legislature changed the death penalty, giving inmates a choice of gas or injection. Any inmate who did not make a choice within 10 days after the execution date was set would be put to death by lethal gas.

The plaintiffs were prisoners of California who had been sentenced to death. They challenged the method of their future executions, asserting that death by lethal gas violates the Eighth Amendment's prohibition against cruel and unusual punishment. Plaintiffs sought a temporary restraining order preventing their executions by administration of lethal gas, the legally prescribed method in California. After consideration of the submissions of the parties and the arguments put forth at the hearing of April 18, 1992 the court under Judge Patel granted plaintiffs' motion.

California's gas chamber had been shut down since 1994, when U.S. District Judge Marilyn Hall Patel in San Francisco ruled that death by gas is an inhumane execution. In 1993, Patel held an eight-day trial, hearing the testimony of several expert medical witnesses and reviewing stacks of scientific literature on the effect of cyanide gas inhalation on humans and animals. In October 1994, Patel ruled that the gas chamber is an inhumane form of punishment and barred the state from using it as a method of execution. California's governor complained that "California should not be prohibited from using the gas chamber to perform executions to society's most brutal and heinous killers."

The state appealed Patel's ruling to the U.S. Court of Appeals in San Francisco. While the state appealed Patel's ruling, prison officials were barred from using the gas chamber. The decision, written by Judge Harry Pregerson, concurred with Patel's finding that death in the gas chamber is extraordinarily painful. Patel's findings of "extreme pain, the length of time this extreme pain lasts, and the substantial risk that the inmate will suffer from this extreme pain for several minutes require the conclusion that execution by lethal gas is cruel and unusual," Pregerson wrote. California argued that eye witness accounts of gas chamber executions, including those of medical professionals who examined the bodies of the deceased, were not competent evidence of the fact the death by lethal gas is slow, painful and torturous, it is unclear to the court what other evidence could be more probative.

The appellate court found that the evidence submitted by plaintiffs suggests strongly that lethal gas may be slow, painful, and torturous in violation of the Eighth Amendment. Judge Pregerson was joined in his decision by Judges Melvin Brunetti and Thomas Nelson.[231] The lower court ruling was then upheld by the U.S. Ninth Circuit Court of Appeals in February 1996. By a 2-to-1 vote, the U.S. Court of Appeals in San Francisco ruled that condemned prisoners have the option of choosing to die either by lethal injection or by gas in San Quentin's death chamber.[232]

In oral argument, the State asserted that because plaintiffs' requested relief would prevent the state from performing executions under its current statutory scheme, plaintiffs claim challenges the very fact of the sentence of execution. When the court granted injunctive relief in this case, the state was not be enjoined from performing executions, but was merely be enjoined from performing executions in an unconstitutional manner. The fact was that the plaintiffs may not be executed by the state's

---

[231] Chiang, Harriet, in *Los Angeles Chronicle,* 22 February 1996; also Weinstein, Henry in *Los Angeles Times,* 22 February 1996.
[232] *Fierro v. Gomez,* 790 F. Supp. 966 (1996)

designated method of execution which was held to be unconstitutional does not prevent the state from carrying out the execution by a constitutionally acceptable means.

## Electrocution

Although each of the following states has chosen lethal injection as the primary method of execution, these states allow electrocution: Alabama, Arkansas, Florida, Kentucky, Mississippi, Oklahoma, South Carolina, Tennessee, and Virginia. The supreme courts of Georgia (2001) and Nebraska (2008) have ruled that the use of the electric chair violates their state constitutional prohibitions against cruel and unusual punishment.

New York built the first electric chair in 1888 and executed William Kemmler in 1890. Other states adopted this method of execution as a more merciful alternative to hanging. Today, electrocution is not used as the sole method of execution in any state, the case again having been made that there is a less painful method of execution available. For execution by the electric chair, the person is usually shaved and strapped to a chair with belts that cross his chest, groin, legs, and arms. A metal skullcap-shaped electrode is attached to the scalp and forehead over a sponge moistened with saline. The sponge must not be too wet or the saline short-circuits the electric current, and not too dry, as it would then have a very high resistance. An additional electrode is moistened with a conductive jelly and attached to a portion of the prisoner's leg that has been shaved to reduce resistance to electricity. The prisoner is then blindfolded. After the execution team has withdrawn to the observation room, the warden signals the executioner, who pulls a handle to connect the power supply which dispenses jolt of between 500 and 2000 volts, which lasts for about 30 seconds. The current surges and is then turned off, at which time the body is seen to relax. The attending physicians wait a few seconds for the body to cool down and then check to see if the inmate's heart is still beating. If it is, another jolt is applied. This process continues until the prisoner is declared dead.

On May 3, 1946, Willie Francis was scheduled to be executed by electrocution in Louisiana. However, the electric chair was improperly setup. When the switch was flipped to execute Francis, execution failed and he moved violently in the chair, is a case in which the U.S. Supreme Court was asked whether imposing capital punishment (the electric chair) a second time, after it failed in an attempt to execute Willie Francis in 1946, constituted a violation of the United States Constitution. King[233] The issues raised surrounded the double jeopardy clause of the 5th Amendment, and the cruel and unusual punishment clause of the 8th Amendment, as made applicable to the State of Louisiana via the due process clause of the 14th Amendment.[234]

Justice Stanley Forman Reed wrote the opinion of the court which held that re-executing Francis did not constitute double jeopardy or cruel and unusual punishment. Three other justices, Chief Justice Vinson and Associate Justices Hugo Black, Robert H. Jackson.

William Francis Kemmler was convicted of killing his common law wife with a hatchet. He was tried and convicted of murder on May 10, 1889. On May 13 he was sentenced to death. New York had instituted death by electrocution. Kemmler's sentence was to be carried out at New York's Auburn Prison using the new electric chair. Kemmler's lawyers appealed, arguing that electrocution was cruel and unusual punishment.[235] The Supreme Court ruled,

> Undoubtedly the amendment forbids any arbitrary deprivation of life, liberty, or property, and secures equal protection to all under like circumstances in the enjoyment of their rights; and, in the administration of criminal justice, requires that no different or higher punishment shall be imposed upon one than is imposed upon all for like offenses. But it was not designed to interfere with the power of the state to protect the lives, liberties, and property of its citizens, and to promote their health, peace, morals, education, and good order. The enactment of this statute was, in itself, within the

---

[233] King, Gilbert, *The Execution of Willie Francis: Race, Murder, and the Search for Justice in the American South*, New York: Basic Civitas, 2008

[234] *Louisiana ex rel. Francis v. Resweber*, 329 U.S. 459 (1947). This case became known as "The Boy Who Was Executed Twice"

[235] *in re Kemmler*, 136 U.S. 436 (1890)

> legitimate sphere of the legislative power of the state, and in the observance of those general rules prescribed by our systems of jurisprudence; and the legislature of the state of New York determined that it did not inflict cruel and unusual punishment, and its courts have sustained that determination. We cannot perceive that the state has thereby abridged the privileges or immunities of the petitioner, or deprived him of due process of law.[236]
>
> Execution required two separate jolts of electricity and took over eight minutes to effect. It was an inauspicious beginning for what became the preferred method of implementing capital punishment. A newspaper judged it infinitely worse than hanging.[237]

A decision of the Supreme Court of Georgia condemned use of electrocution. That court held as follows: The people of Georgia chose electrocution as the method of executing persons sentenced to death for capital offenses. The State Supreme Court operated from the presumption that this method of execution is constitutional. However, that presumption of constitutionality cannot prevail when a statute manifestly infringes upon a constitutional provision or violates the rights of the people. Thus, the mere fact that the Legislature has spoken on the issue of the method of execution does not preclude or in any manner limit this Court's evaluation of the selected method to determine whether it comports with the constitutional prohibition against cruel and unusual punishment. The General Assembly later decided that condemned persons be executed by lethal injection because electrocution violates the Constitution of Georgia.

Both state and defense experts, electrocution survivors, and prison officials, as well as autopsy reports prepared by the State after Georgia executions, audiotapes archiving Georgia executions, postmortem photographs of persons executed in Georgia suggest that electrocution produces great suffering. One defense expert testified that there is a possibility, even a likelihood, that Georgia's electric chair does not produce instantaneous unconsciousness. The defense expert further

---

[236] *in re Kemmler*, 136 U.S. 436 at 438 (1890)
[237] "Far Worse Than Hanging" *New York Times*. August 7, 1890.

claimed that the alternating current used in electrocutions could repetitively activate the brain, causing the perception of excruciating pain and a sense of extreme horror. Another defense expert testified that the two high-voltage portions of the electrocution process, which last a total of eleven seconds, would induce cardiac standstill but that the third, low-voltage portion of the electrocution process, which lasts 109 seconds, might fail to produce its designed effect of inducing ventricular fibrillation in half of all executions.

The court found that in two instances documented by prison officials as a record of Georgia executions, a second two-minute cycle of electricity was required due to life signs exhibited by the prisoner. In one case, breathing was observed during the five-minute "cooling off" period following the initial two-minute application of electricity, thus requiring the application of another two-minute cycle of electricity. In another case, the prisoner was observed bobbing his head from side to side during both the low-voltage portion of the first two-minute electrocution cycle and the five-minute lapse period that followed. The physicians who examined the prisoner during the first five-minute lapse period determined that he was still breathing. Although the prisoner stopped moving his head when the second cycle of electricity was initiated, the head movements resumed and he appeared to be breathing during both the final portion of the second electrocution cycle and during the first two minutes of the second cooling-off period. Autopsy reports and autopsy photographs prepared as part of the State's execution protocol establish that some degree of burning of the prisoner's body is present in every electrocution. The autopsy reports contain repeated comments to the effect that the burns found on the deceased prisoners are "characteristic" or "typical" of injuries observed in previous executions, and there are references to blisters and burn marks observed on other places on the bodies. The autopsies also reference the sloughing or "slippage" of a large portion of the scalp and the skin at the back of the head and also on the legs caused by the execution.

The Georgia high court concluded the following regarding execution by electrocution. "This Court granted Dawson and Moore's applications for interim review, consolidated the cases, and directed the parties to address whether electrocution remains a constitutional method of execution in Georgia. Upon considered review of this difficult issue, we conclude that future use of electrocution as a means of executing death sentences in Georgia would violate the prohibition against cruel and unusual punishment in Art. I, Sec. I, Par. XVII of the Georgia Constitution. Therefore, we direct that any future executions of death sentences in Georgia be carried out by lethal injection in accordance with O.C.G.A. § 17-10-38, as amended."[238]

Morris Thigpen, Alabama Prison Commissioner, admitted that it took two jolts of electricity, nine minutes apart, to complete the 1989 execution of Horace Franklin Dunkins, Jr. Because someone had improperly placed the cables, it was impossible to administer sufficient current to cause death. A guard had the most unpleasant job of adjusting and reconnecting the cables before a second jolt could be administered. Death was pronounced 19 minutes after the first electric charge.

## Firing Squad

In 2015 Utah reinstated the firing squad as a legal method of executing condemned prisoners. The law only allows Utah to use a firing squad if the chemicals required for lethal injection are unavailable, which is not an impossible scenario, given that many companies that manufacture such chemicals are refusing to sell them to prisons because they do not want to be associated with executions. Oklahoma allows the use of a firing squad only in the cases where lethal injection drugs are unavailable.

Utah authorized use of a firing squad as a viable method of execution only if the state was unable to obtain the drugs necessary to carry out a lethal injection execution. The most recent execution by this method was Ronnie Gardner who consciously chose this method. The inmate is typically bound to a chair with leather straps across his waist and head, in front of an oval-shaped canvas wall. The chair is surrounded by sandbags to absorb the bullets that pass through the inmate and to absorb the inmate's blood. A black hood is pulled over the inmate's head. The attending physician pins a circular white cloth target over the heart. Standing in an enclosure 20 feet away, five shooters are armed with 30/30

---

[238] *Dawson v. State,* 274 Ga. 327, 327-328 (2001)

caliber rifles loaded with single rounds, although one of the shooters is given a blank round. Each of the shooters aims his rifle through a slot in the canvas and fires at the inmate. The prisoner dies as a result of blood loss caused by rupture of the heart or a large blood vessel, or tearing of the lungs. The person shot loses consciousness when shock causes a fall in the supply of blood to the brain. It is most unlikely that the four shooters using ammunition will miss the heart.

The first known and reported execution in America was carried out by firing squad. In 1608, George Kendall was shot for a mutinous plot, also in Jamestown, Virginia, perhaps spying for Spain, although details of the case are unknown.[239] Hangings during the colonial era of America were mostly performed publicly in order to deter the behavior for which the criminals were hanged. Thousands of townspeople would gather around the gallows to hear a sermon and observe the hangings of convicted criminals. Such experiences were deemed to be good lessons on morality for the children.

The earliest court hearing involving the imposition of the death penalty by hanging, the *Wilkerson* Case, originated in Utah. That state enacted a law on March 6, 1862, which stated that a person convicted of a capital offense "shall suffer death by being shot, hanged, or beheaded," decided by the court, or "he shall have his option as to the manner of his execution." In 1877 Wallace Wilkerson was charged with premeditated murder for killing William Baxter and was sentenced to die. He was given a choice of execution between decapitation, hanging, and firing squad; Wilkerson elected to be executed by firing squad. The following year, Wilkerson appealed to the Supreme Court of Utah territory on the grounds that execution by firing squad presented unnecessary cruelty and unusual punishment. While using a firing squad was permissible the courts found that old English practices such as a prisoner being disemboweled alive, beheaded, or being burned alive were ruled unconstitutional.[240]

---

[239] Espy, Watt and Smykla John Ortiz. *The Espy Files*. This is the standard database of executions carried out in the United States and preceding territories from 1608, which is the most complete source of data on the issue, identifying 15,487 people put to death.

[240] *Wilkerson v. Utah*, 99 U.S. 130 (1879)

Congress made no regulations regarding methods of execution for either American territories or the military, the custom of war, says a learned writer upon the subject, has, in the absence of statutory law, determined that capital punishment be inflicted by shooting or hanging; and the same author adds to the effect that mutiny, meaning mutiny not resulting in loss of life, desertion, or other military crime, if a capital offense, is commonly punished by shooting; that a spy is always hanged, and that mutiny, if accompanied by loss of life, is punished in the same manner,—that is, by hanging. General military laws do not say how a criminal offending against such laws shall be put to death, but leave it entirely to the custom of war. Shooting or hanging are the standard methods determined by the custom. Mutiny unaccompanied with loss of life is punished by the same means; and desertion, disobedience of orders, or other capital crimes are usually punished by shooting, adding, that the mode in all cases, that is, either shooting or hanging, may be declared upon the imposition of sentence.[241]

## Lethal Injections

The following states allow or mandate the use of lethal injections: Alabama, Arizona, Arkansas, California, Colorado, Florida, Georgia, Idaho, Indiana, Kansas, Kentucky, Louisiana, Mississippi, Missouri, Montana, Nebraska, Nevada, New Hampshire, New Mexico, North Carolina, Ohio, Oklahoma, Oregon, Pennsylvania, South Carolina, South Dakota, Tennessee, Texas, Utah, Virginia, and Wyoming. Delaware and Washington have declared their capital sentencing procedures unconstitutional and have re-sentenced all death-row prisoners to life without parole. New Mexico abolished the death penalty but the repeal may not apply retroactively, leaving prisoners on death row facing possible execution. At the federal level lethal injections are used by the U.S. Military, as well as the U.S. Government.

---

[241]Macomb, Alexander, *The Practice of Courts Martial*. New York: Harper & Brothers, 1841; see also Benét, Stephen Vincent (1827-1895). *A Treatise on Military Law and the Practice of Courts-Martial*. VanNostrand, 1862); and Simmons, Thomas Frederick. *Remarks on the Constitution and Practice of Courts Martial*. New York, 5th ed., 1863.

Charles Brooks would become the first person executed by lethal injection in Texas on December 2, 1982. As of this date, all of the 32 states that have the death penalty use this method. When this method is used, the condemned person is usually bound to a gurney and a member of the execution team positions several heart monitors on this skin. Two needles, one being a back-up, are then inserted into usable veins, usually in the inmate's arms. Long tubes connect the needle through a hole in a cement block wall to several intravenous drips. The first is a harmless saline solution that is started immediately. Then, at the warden's signal, a curtain is raised exposing the inmate to the witnesses in an adjoining room. Then, the inmate is injected with sodium thiopental - an anesthetic, which puts the inmate to sleep. Next flows pavulon or pancuronium bromide, which paralyzes the entire muscle system and stops the inmate's breathing. Finally, the flow of potassium chloride stops the heart. Death results from anesthetic overdose and respiratory and cardiac arrest while the condemned person is unconscious. Medical ethics preclude physicians from participating in executions of criminals even though the same ethics allow partial-birth abortions. However, it is necessary that a licensed physician will certify the inmate is dead.

Ralph Baze and Thomas Bowling were sentenced to death in Kentucky, each for a double-murder. They argued that executing them by lethal injection would violate the Eighth Amendment. Partially because of botched executions using this method, there was strong opinion that lethal injection must not inflict "unnecessary pain." Plaintiffs argued that the lethal chemicals that Kentucky used carried a significant risk of inflicting pain during the execution. Kentucky at the time used the then-common combination of sodium thiopental, pancuronium bromide, and potassium chloride. The Supreme Court of Kentucky had rejected their claim, but the U.S. Supreme Court granted *certiorari*.

The case had nationwide implications because the specific combination of drugs that Kentucky used for lethal injections was essentially the same one that virtually all states used for lethal injection. The U.S. Supreme Court stayed all executions in the country between September 2007 and April 2008, when it delivered its ruling and affirmed the Kentucky Supreme Court's decision by a 7-2 vote, thus allowing executions to proceed.[242]

Activists who opposed the death-penalty then pressured pharmaceutical companies to prevent sodium thiopental (and, later, another barbiturate called pentobarbital) from being used in executions. Unable to obtain either sodium thiopental or pentobarbital, Oklahoma decided to use a 500-milligram dose of midazolam, a sedative, as the first drug in its three-drug protocol.

On April 29, 2014, Oklahoma used midazolam in the execution of Clayton Lockett. After executioners had performed the lethal injection, Lockett began to struggle on the gurney, reportedly groaning "the drugs aren't working." It took Lockett died forty-three minutes to die after the lethal mixture was injected. After an investigation, Oklahoma elected to continue using midazolam in executions. [243] On June 25, 2014, Warner, Glossip, and nineteen other Oklahoma death row inmates sued in the United States District Court for the Western District of Oklahoma, alleging Oklahoma's use of midazolam violated the Eighth Amendment to the United States Constitution. Four of those inmates filed a motion for a preliminary injunction and argued that a 500-milligram dose of midazolam will not render them unable to feel pain associated with administration of the second and third drugs. The District Court denied the motion in part because the prisoners had failed to identify a known and available alternative method of execution that presented a substantially less severe risk of pain. It also held that the prisoners failed to establish a likelihood of showing that the use of midazolam created a demonstrated risk of severe pain. The petitioners failed to establish that any risk of harm was substantial when compared to a known and available alternative method of execution. Oklahoma presented expert testimony that a 500-milligram dose of midazolam would make it a virtual certainty that an inmate will not feel pain associated with the second and third drugs. The experts hired by the petitioners acknowledged that they had no proof to the contrary. U.S. District Judge Stephen P. Friot orally denied the condemned prisoners'

---

[242] *Baze v. Rees,* 553 U.S. 35 (2008)

[243] Stern, Jeffrey "The Cruel and Unusual Execution of Clayton Lockett," *Atlantic,* June 2015.

request for a preliminary injunction prohibiting the use of midazolam in their executions. On January 12, 2015, Tenth Circuit Judge Mary Beck Briscoe, joined by Neil Gorsuch and Scott Matheson Jr., affirmed.[244]

The case then went to the Supreme Court. During the oral arguments, four conservative justices expressed impatience with the obstructionist attitude of plaintiffs' attorneys. Justice Scalia reasoned that the real cause of the delay in executions had been caused "by the abolitionists putting pressure on the companies that manufacture" the best choice drugs. Justice Alito called this "guerrilla war against the death penalty." Four liberal justices questioned the Oklahoma Solicitor General, with Justice Kagan describing the execution protocol as "burning alive, from the inside."[245] Justice Alito delivered the opinion of the sharply divided Court. By a 5-4 vote the U.S. Supreme Court affirmed Oklahoma's position.[246]

The major problem in recent years has been the refusal of drug companies and suppliers to sell the chemicals necessary to execute criminals by lethal injection. Fearing reaction from the public as well as stockholders many corporations have refused the sale or manufacture of recommended drugs.

Cormac McCarthy (1933--) is an American novelist, playwright, and screenwriter. He has written ten novels, spanning the Southern Gothic, Western, and post-apocalyptic genres. He has won both the National Book Award and National Book Critics Circle Award. McCarthy described a prolonged execution by lethal injection:

> Robert Waterhouse was scheduled for execution at
> 6:00pm this evening. In accordance with the established
> execution protocol he was strapped to the gurney and the
> needles were inserted into each arm about 45 minutes

---

[244] *Warner v. Gross*, 776 F.3d 721 (10th Cir. 2015).

[245] Liptak, Adam. "Justices Approve Execution Drug in a 5-to-4 Vote - A Sharp Clash of Views - Two in Dissent Question Constitutionality of the Death Penalty" *New York Times,* 30 June 2015; See also Lithwick, Dahlia. "A Horrifying Day at Court: Death brings out the worst in the justices". *Slate,* 30 April 2015.

[246] *Glossip v. Gross*, 135 S.Ct. 2726 (2015)

prior to his appointed time. Just before 6:00, however, he received a 45-minute stay which morphed into an almost 3-hour endurance test as he remained on the gurney as the seconds, minutes and then hours slid by at an excruciatingly slow pace, waiting for someone to tell him if hope was at hand, if he would live or die. Just before 9:00 he received his answer, the plungers were depressed, the syringes emptied and he was summarily killed. Here on the row we can discern the approximate time of death when we see the old white Cadillac hearse trundle in through the back sally port gate to pick up the body, the same familiar 1960's era hearse I've watched for almost 40 years, coming in to retrieve the bodies of murdered prisoners, which used to happen on a regular basis back when I was in open population. I've seen a lot of guys, both friends and foes, carted off in that old hearse. Anyway, pause for a moment to imagine being on that gurney for over three hours, the needles in your arms. You've already come to terms with your imminent death, you are reconciled with the reality that this is it, this is how you will die, that there will be no reprieve. Then, at the last moment, a cruel trick, you're given that slim hope, which you instinctively grasp. Some court, somewhere, has given you a temporary stay. You stare at the ceiling while the clock on the wall ticks away. You are totally alone, not a friendly soul in sight, surrounded by grim-faced men who are determined to kill you. Your heart pounds, your body feels electrified and every second seems like an eternity as a Kaleidoscope of wild thoughts crash around frantically in your compressed mind. After 3 hours you are drained, exhausted, terrorized, and then the phone on the wall rings and you're told it's time to die. . . ."[247]

---

[247] McCarthy, Cormac. *The Road.* New York: Vintage, 2007

# Bibliography

Alphin, Elaine Marie. *An Unspeakable Crime: The Prosecution and Persecution of Leo Frank.* Carolrhoda Books, 2010.

Applebome, Peter "Death Penalty; Arkansas Execution Raises Questions on Governor's Politics", *New York Times*, 25 January 1992

Arnett, Jeffrey, "Reckless Behavior in Adolescence: A Developmental Perspective," *Developmental Review,* 12: 339-73 (1992).

*The assassination of Abraham Lincoln, late President of the United States of America and the attempted assassination of William H. Seward, Secretary of State, and Frederick W. Seward, Assistant Secretary, on the evening of the 14th of April, 1865.* Washington: Government Printing Office, 1867.

Barnes, R. "Supreme Court finds Florida's capital punishment process unconstitutional," *Washington Post*, January 12, 2016

Bazelon, Emily, "The Death Penalty Just Got a Tiny Bit Saner: Today's Supreme Court Decision Makes It Harder for States to Execute the Mentally Disabled." *Slate,* 27 May 2014.

Billotte, Jamie M. "Is It Justified - The Death Penalty and Mental Retardation", *Notre Dame J. L. Ethics & Pub. Pol'y* 8: 333 (1994).

Bing, Jonathan L. "Protecting the Mentally Retarded from Capital Punishment: State Efforts Since Penry and Recommendations for the Future". N.Y.U. Review of Law & Social Change. 22 : 1 at 59–151 (1996).

Blumenthal, Ralph. "A Growing Plea for Mercy for the Mentally Ill on Death Row." *New York Times*, 23 November 2006.

Bordenave, F. and Kelly, D. "Death Penalty and Mentally Ill Defendants," *Journal of the American Academy of Psychiatry and the Law,* (2010).

Brigham, John. "Unusual Punishment: The Federal Death Penalty in the United States." *Washington University Journal of Law & Policy.* January 2004. Volume 16 (Access to Justice: The Social Responsibility of Lawyers | New Federalism). p. 195-233

Byrne, William A, "Slave Crime in Savannah, Georgia" *The Journal of Negro*

*History*, Vol. 79, [1994].

Carter, Dan T., *Scottsboro: A Tragedy of the American South*, revised ed. Baton Rouge: Louisiana State University Press, 1979.

Carmichael, Virginia. *Framing History: the Rosenberg Story and the Cold War.* University of Minnesota Press, 1993.

Carter, Dan. "And the Dead Shall Rise: The Murder of Mary Phagan and the Lynching of Leo Frank". *Journal of Southern History*, Vol. 71, Issue 2 (May 2005).

Casto, William R., *The Supreme Court in the Early Republic: The Chief Justiceships of John Jay and Oliver Ellsworth*, University of South Carolina Press, 1995.

Clune, Lori, *Executing the Rosenbergs: Death and Diplomacy in a Cold War World* Oxford University Press, 2016.

Cooke, Brian K., Delalot, Dominque and Werner, Tonia L. "Hall v. Florida: Capital Punishment, IQ, and Persons With Intellectual Disabilities" *Journal of the American Academy of Psychiatry and the Law Online*, 43: 2 at 230-234 (June 2015).

Dalton, Laura. "Stanford v. Kentucky and Wilkins v. Missouri: A Violation of an Emerging Rule of Customary International Law," 32 *Wm. & Mary L. Rev.* 161 (1990).

Edwards, William C.; Steers, Edward, eds. *The Lincoln Assassination: The Evidence*. University of Illinois Press, 2010.

Elliott, Carl. *The Rules of Insanity: Moral Responsibility and the Mentally Ill Offender.* SUNY Press, 1996.

Emshwiller, J and Audi, T, "Loughner's Mental Competence is Doubted," *Wall Street Journal*, 17 May 2011.

Entzeroth, Lyn. "Constitutional Prohibition on the Execution of the Mentally Retarded Criminal Defendant," *Tulsa L. Rev.* 38: 299 (2013).

Erikson, Erik, *Identity, Youth and Crisis*. New York: Norton, 1968.

Foner, Philip S. and Herbert Shapiro, eds., *American Communism and Black Americans: A Documentary History, 1930–1934* Philadelphia: Temple University Press, 1991.

Franklin, K. "Loughner Case Shines Spotlight on Forced Meds Practices," *Forensic Psychology, Criminology, and Psychology-law*, 10 July 2011.

Freedman, Allison. "Mental Retardation and the Death Penalty: The Need for an International Standard Defining Mental Retardation," 12 *N W. J. Int'l Hum. Rts.* 1 (2014);

Goldstein, J. and Lacey, M. "To Defend the Accused in a Tucson Rampage, First a Battle to Get Inside a Mind," *New York Times*, 12 February 2011.

Grosso, Catherine and O'Brien, Barbara, "A Stubborn Legacy: The Overwhelming Importance of Race in Jury Selection in 173 Post-*Batson* North

Carolina Capital Trials," 97 *Iowa L. Rev.* 1531 (2012).

Hagenah, Patricia (1990). "Imposing the Death Sentence on Mentally Retarded Defendants: The Case of Penry v. Lynaugh". *UMKC Law Review.* 59: 1 at 135–153 (1990).

Henson, Burt M., and Ross R. Olney. *Furman v. Georgia: The Death Penalty and the Constitution.* New York: Franklin Watts, 1996.

Herda, D.J. *Furman v. Georgia: The Death Penalty Case.* Enslow Publishers, 1994.

Hornblum, Allen M. *The Invisible Harry Gold: The Man Who Gave the Soviets the Atom Bomb.* Yale University Press 2010.

Howard, Peter. *Female Serial Killers: How and Why Women Become Monsters.* New York: Penguin, 2007, pp.142-43.

Hufbauer, Gary Clyde; Mitrokostas, Nicholas K. (2004). "International Implications of the Alien Tort Statute." 16 *St. Thomas L. Rev.* 607 (2004).J

ones, Stephen and Peter Israel. *Others Unknown: Timothy McVeigh and the Oklahoma City* Bombing Conspiracy, 2nd ed. New York: PublicAffairs, 2001.

Kaplan, John, and Robert Weisberg. *Criminal Law: Cases and Materials.* 2d ed. Boston: Little, Brown, 1991.

Klarman, Michael J. "The Racial Origins of Modern Criminal Procedure".*Mich. L. Rev.* 99: 1, 48–97 (2000)

.Madeira, Jody Lyneé. *Killing McVeigh: The Death Penalty and the Myth of Closure.* New York University Press, 2012.

Miller, Kent S. and Radelet, Michael L. *Executing the Mentally Ill: The Criminal Justice System and the Case of Alvin Ford.* London: Sage, 1990.

O'Sullivan, Carol. *The Death Penalty: Identifying Propaganda Techniques.* San Diego: Greenhaven Press, 1989.

Paternoster, Raymond. *Capital Punishment in America.* New York: Lexington, 1991.

Phillips, Ulrich B., "Slave Crime in Virginia." *American Historical Review* 20 [January 1915]: 336-40.

Pollitt, Daniel R. and Warren, Brittany P., "Thirty Years of Disappointment: North Carolina's Remarkable Appellate *Batson* Record", 94 *N.C. L. Rev.* 1957 (2016).

*Report of the Trial and Conviction of John Haggerty for the murder of Melchior Fordney, Late of the City of Lancaster, Pennsylvania: in the Court of Oyer & Terminer, Held at the City of Lancaster, for the County of Lancaster, at January term, A.D. 1847. Before the Hon. Ellis Lewis, President and Jacob Grosh und Emanuel Schaeffer Associate Justices of Said Court. Lancaster,* 1847. 82 pp.

Rizzo, T. "Missouri Lawyers Say Man on Death Row is Mentally Incompetent Because of Sawmill Accident," *Kansas City Star,* 8 March 2015.

Schmidt, Benno C., Jr., "Juries, Jurisdiction, and Race Discrimination: The Lost

Promise of *Strauder v. West Virginia*," *Texas L. Rev.* 61: 1401 (1983).

Rogers, John M., "The Alien Tort Statute and How Individuals Violate International Law," 21 *Vand. J. Transnat'l Law* 47 (1988).

Scholnick, Myron L., *Journal of Southern History,* Vol. 61, No. 4 (November 1995), pp. 860–861.

Silvio, Heather; McCloskey, Kathy; and Ramos-Grenier, Julia. "Theoretical Consideration of Female Sexual Predator Serial Killers in the United States". *Journal of Criminal Justice.* 34: 3, 251–259 (2006).

Simmons, Susan M. "Thompson v. Oklahoma: Debating the Constitutionality of Juvenile Executions," 16 *Pepp. L. Rev.* 3 (1989).

Speed, Attorney General James, *Opinion on the constitutional power of the military to try and execute the assassins of the President.* Washington: Government Printing Office, 1865

Stack, Richard A. *Dead Wrong: Violence, Vengeance, and the Victims of Capital Punishment.* Greenwood Publishing Group, 2006.

Steers Jr., Edward, and Holzer, Harold, eds. *The Lincoln Assassination Conspirators: Their Confinement and Execution, as Recorded in the Letterbook of John Frederick Hartranft.* Louisiana State University Press, 2009.

Steinberg, Laurence & Scott, Elizabeth, "Less Guilty by Reason of Adolescence: Developmental Immaturity, Diminished Responsibility, and the Juvenile Death Penalty", *American Psychologist* 58: 1009.

Stephens, William, ed. *Proceedings in Georgia,* Ann Arbor: University of Michigan, 1966, 2 vols.

Stone, Alan. "Condemned Prisoner Treated and Executed," *Psychiatric Times,* March 2004.

Tirschwell, Eric A. and Theodore Hertzberg. "Politics and Prosecutions: A Historical Perspective on Shifting Federal Standards for Pursuing the Death Penalty in non-Death Penalty States." *Journal of Constitutional Law.* October 2009. Volume 12 Issue 1. p. 57-98.

Vattel, Emmerich. *The Law of Nations; Or, Principles of the Law of Nature, Applied to the Conduct and Affairs of Nations and Sovereigns. A Work Tending to Display the True Interest of Powers.*

Williams, T. "Lawyers Seek Reprieve for Killer Who Lost Part of His Brain Decades Earlier," *New York Times,* 7 March 2015.

# Index